C000183963

ITIL® 4 Create, Deliver and Support (CDS)

Your companion to the ITIL 4 Managing Professional CDS certification

ITIL® 4 Create, Deliver and Support (CDS)

Your companion to the ITIL 4 Managing
Professional CDS certification

CLAIRE AGUTTER

IT Governance Publishing

Every possible effort has been made to ensure that the information contained in this book is accurate at the time of going to press, and the publisher and the author cannot accept responsibility for any errors or omissions, however caused. Any opinions expressed in this book are those of the author, not the publisher. Websites identified are for reference only, not endorsement, and any website visits are at the reader's own risk. No responsibility for loss or damage occasioned to any person acting, or refraining from action, as a result of the material in this publication can be accepted by the publisher or the author.

ITIL® is a registered trademark of AXELOS Limited. All rights reserved.

Apart from any fair dealing for the purposes of research or private study, or criticism or review, as permitted under the Copyright, Designs and Patents Act 1988, this publication may only be reproduced, stored or transmitted, in any form, or by any means, with the prior permission in writing of the publisher or, in the case of reprographic reproduction, in accordance with the terms of licences issued by the Copyright Licensing Agency. Enquiries concerning reproduction outside those terms should be sent to the publisher at the following address:

IT Governance Publishing Ltd
Unit 3, Clive Court
Bartholomew's Walk
Cambridgeshire Business Park
Ely, Cambridgeshire
CB7 4EA
United Kingdom
www.itgovernancepublishing.co.uk

© Claire Agutter 2021

The author has asserted the rights of the author under the Copyright, Designs and Patents Act, 1988, to be identified as the author of this work.

First edition published in the United Kingdom in 2021 by IT Governance Publishing

ISBN 978-1-78778-337-9

ABOUT THE AUTHOR

Claire Agutter is a service management trainer, consultant and author. In 2020, she was one of Computer Weekly's Top 50 Most Influential Women in Tech. In 2018 and 2019, she was recognised as an HDI Top 25 Thought Leader and was part of the team that won itSMF UK's 2017 Thought Leadership Award. Claire provides regular, free content to the IT service management (ITSM) community as the host of the popular ITSM Crowd hangouts, and is the chief architect for VeriSM™, the service management approach for the digital age. Claire is the director of ITSM Zone, which provides online IT service management training, and Scopism. She has worked with ITGP to publish *Service Integration and Management (SIAM™) Foundation Body of Knowledge (BoK), Second edition* and *Service Integration and Management (SIAM™) Professional Body of Knowledge (BoK), Second edition*, the official guides for the EXIN SIAM™ Foundation and Professional certifications.

After providing support to thousands of people taking ITIL training and certification from version 2 onwards, she has created this series of books for those studying towards ITIL 4 Managing Professional and Strategic Leader status.

For more information, please visit:

- *https://itsm.zone*
- *www.scopism.com*

Contact:

- *www.linkedin.com/in/claireagutter/*

- *https://twitter.com/ClaireAgutter*

For more information about Claire's other publications with ITGP, visit:

www.itgovernancepublishing.co.uk/author/claire-agutter

CONTENTS

Contents

Contents

Contents

Contents

INTRODUCTION

How to use this book

The majority of this book is based on the *ITIL® 4: Create, Deliver and Support* publication and the associated ITIL® 4 Specialist Create, Deliver and Support syllabus.

The *ITIL® 4: Create, Deliver and Support* publication describes how to *"make service management work, how to adapt and adopt best practices, and how to make the Service Value System a reality for your organization."*

CDS is described as the 'glue' of the service lifecycle and focuses on how service management delivers value. Value itself is a moving target – what is valuable today may not be tomorrow. The key themes related to create, deliver and support and its supporting management practices are the focus of the CDS publication and associated training and examination.

In this companion to the CDS syllabus, in addition to helping you prepare for your certification, I want to give you advice and guidance that will lead to you using this book once your training and exam are complete. I have added some of my own practical experience and give advice and points to think about along the way. My goal is for you to refer back to this book in years to come, not just put it away once you've passed your exam. With this extra content, you'll find this book is an excellent supplement to any training course and a useful resource in your ongoing career.

As you read the book, assume that all the content is related to the syllabus unless it is highlighted in one of two ways:

Something for you: a small exercise for you to complete to apply the ITIL 4 concepts in your own role, or a point for you to think about. This content is not examinable.

Practical experiences: any content marked out with this image is based on my own experience and is not examinable.

The content highlighted as something for you to think about or practical experience might also refer to the Banksbest case study you can find in Appendix A. I'll use the case study to give an example of how something would work in the real world, or to help you apply what you're reading about. Case studies can really help to bring abstract concepts to life. The case study is not examinable but using it will help you gain a deeper understanding of the CDS concepts. Let's start with something for you now:

Why not read the case study and make a note of your first impressions of the Banksbest organisation and its plans before you start to study the CDS content in this book?

Unless stated otherwise, all quotations are from *ITIL® 4 Create, Deliver and Support* and *Practice Guides* published by AXELOS in 2020. Copyright © AXELOS Limited 2020. Used under permission of AXELOS Limited. All rights reserved.

CHAPTER 1: SERVICE VALUE SYSTEM KEY CONCEPTS AND CHALLENGES

The first chapters in this book look at how to plan and build a service value system (SVS) to create, deliver and support services. This includes:

- Understanding the concepts and challenges relating to the SVS;
- Understanding how to use a 'shift-left' approach;
- Knowing how to plan and manage resources in the SVS; and
- Understanding the use and value of information and technology across the SVS.

This information provides the foundation for the activities and choices practitioners and managers can use as services are created, delivered and supported.

SVS concepts and challenges: Organisational structure

The way an organisation is structured will have an impact on how it works. Structure affects how people work together, how decisions are made, and how new ideas are shared.

Table 1: Organisation Structures

Functional	Functional structures are typically hierarchical, with defined formal lines of authority, clear roles and responsibilities, and clear allocation of power and responsibility.

	Examples of functions could be sales, finance, IT, etc.
Divisional	Divisional structures are based around organisational entities such as markets, products or geographical areas. In a divisional structure, each division may operate as an individual entity with its own profit and loss, support teams, etc.
Matrix	A matrix structure occurs when staff have dual reporting lines; for example, to a line manager and a product manager for a piece of work. Matrix organisations are represented as a grid of relationships, and often describe 'pools' of people who can move between projects and products. They can support more agile ways of working and rapid reconfiguration of resources.
Flat	Flat organisations have very little hierarchy and can support fast decision-making by enabling autonomy. This may, however, create challenges as an organisation grows.

Think about the structure or your current, or most recent, employer. Does it fall into one of these types? What benefits did the organisational structure offer? Did it create any challenges?

The key differences between organisational structures are often defined by:

- Grouping/team basis (e.g. product, function, customer);
- Location – co-located or not;
- Relationship to value streams – responsible for individual step(s) or an entire value stream; and
- Levels of autonomy and authority (command and control vs delegation or self-organising teams).

Digital transformation requires organisations to be more flexible and agile, which has an impact on structure. Matrix structures, resource pools and the ability to use external staff can all offer benefits. Some organisations are moving from project-based to product-based teams to provide consistency and ownership from demand to value. Any change in organisation structure should have appropriate change controls applied.

Take a look at the Banksbest case study and read about the organisation's relationship with Employeez on Demand. This supplier provides extra resources during peak times. What would Banksbest need to consider from a contractual and a service management perspective to ensure its customers receive a good service when they are speaking to Employeez on Demand staff?

SVS concepts and challenges: Integrated/collaborative culture

Collaboration and cooperation are separate concepts that should not be confused. Collaboration requires active and passive participation from all people and groups in the organisation to be effective. Cooperation is often based around goals; a group that is focused solely on its own goal can become a silo as it loses sight of the bigger picture.

For collaboration to take place, goals and key performance indicators (KPIs) for groups need to be shared, integrated, and aligned to organisational goals.

Table 2: Collaboration and Cooperation

Collaboration	Cooperation
Work together towards a shared goal/objective	Separate goals can lead to silo working

Shared and integrated goals	Aligned goals
Everyone succeeds or fails together	Individuals and teams succeed independently
Goals and resources aligned in real time	Cooperative, friendly, willing to share information
Technology is necessary but not sufficient	Technology is necessary but not sufficient
Needs respect, trust and transparency	Less need for trust and transparency
Needs multi-channel communication (stand ups, face-to-face, active listening, tool-mediated, etc.)	Needs effective communication
Everyone needs to understand how they contribute to the big picture	Everyone needs to understand their own role
Need to understand PESTLE* factors for all stakeholders	Need to understand PESTLE factors for own role

* **PESTLE** analysis looks at these factors as part of an analysis:

- Political
- Economical
- Social
- Technological
- Legal
- Environmental

The work that a team does may be classed as algorithmic or heuristic.

Table 3: Algorithmic or Heuristic

Algorithmic tasks	Heuristic tasks
Follow a defined process, with established instructions	Depend on human understanding and intervention
Follow the rules	Learn or discover what is needed
Clear inputs, outputs, instructions, branches, etc.	Need flexibility, information, knowledge and experience
Reassignment and handover between teams where needed	Collaboration, swarming and DevOps often appropriate
People doing the work may recognise opportunities to improve how it is done – this should be part of their role	New insights can be recorded for future use, moving some work to algorithmic (removing 'toil' – manual, repetitive work that is devoid of enduring value. Toil scales in a linear

	way, for example more users equals more password resets.)

Think about your typical working day. How much of your work is pre-planned, and how much just 'happens'? Are your tasks algorithmic or heuristic? Algorithmic tasks may be suitable for automation or improvement, but to identify that, you will also need time to review what you are doing. Teams, for example, that spend much of their time firefighting and carrying out reactive work may struggle to find time to identify ways to do things better.

Collaboration happens within IT teams, as well as with service consumers, service provider employees, shareholders, regulators, partners, suppliers, and any other relevant stakeholders. Whether an organisation offers business-to-business (B2B) or business-to-consumer (B2C) services also has an impact on the stakeholders it will need to collaborate with. Technology (such as Slack or Microsoft Teams) can support collaboration, but don't forget the guiding principle is to collaborate and promote visibility. Don't lose information because it's hidden in a tool.

The digital economy is also imposing new challenges on organisational leaders, as well as organisational structures.

Servant leadership is an approach that allows leaders and managers to focus on supporting rather than directing staff.

Looking back over your career, how many managers have you worked with who have genuinely inspired you? How many senior people have helped you to develop and made you a better person? When I reflect on my career, the number is very small, but I remember those managers for the huge impact that they had on me. Many of the managers who helped me to grow professionally (and personally) displayed servant leadership characteristics. They listened to their people and supported them almost unconditionally. They encouraged me to resolve problems for myself, while providing guidance when it was needed.

Any organisation that wants to thrive in a digital world will be familiar with all of the cultural buzzwords that go along with digital transformation – agility, autonomy, self-directing teams, etc. What is often missed are the leadership and management behaviours that allow this.

SVS concepts and challenges: Teams, roles and competencies

Traditionally, IT roles were focused on areas such as designer, programmer, business analyst or support analyst. Organisations now require staff to be more flexible and able to change their role. Business skills like relationship management, team leadership, negotiation, and supplier and contract management are also required.

ITIL uses a competency profile to describe roles. Remember, the roles that are described in the CDS publication and associated management practices are not mandatory. They shouldn't be treated like a checklist of things that you have to have; instead, they should be adapted to the specific needs of your organisation.

Table 4: Competency Profiles

Leader (L)	*"Decision-making, delegating, overseeing other activities, providing incentives and motivation, and evaluating outcomes."*
Administrator (A)	*"Assigning and prioritizing tasks, record-keeping, ongoing reporting, and initiating basic improvements."*
Coordinator/ Communicator (C)	*"Coordinating multiple parties, maintaining communication between stakeholders, and running awareness campaigns."*
Methods and Techniques Expert (M)	*"Designing and implementing work techniques, documenting procedures, consulting on processes, work analysis, and continual improvement."*

Technical Expert (T)	*"Providing technical (IT) expertise and conducting expertise-based assignments."*

The competencies can be combined to create a profile, for example CAT or TMA. Note that the position of each competency equates to its importance.

Consider the following profiles:

- **CAT**

  CAT describes a relationship manager or a service owner. Both roles require excellent communication and coordination skills and good administrative skills, and technical knowledge is useful.

- **TMA**

  TMA describes a change manager where excellent technical knowledge is critical, an understanding of design method is needed and some administrative skills are also required.

Review Doug's profile in the Banksbest case study. What competencies will he have? Which will be the most useful in his current role?

Why are competency profiles useful? First, they can help to identify the best candidates for a specific role. A profile can highlight gaps in the current capabilities and support plans to alleviate those gaps with new hires or training. It can also create better job/role descriptions and be used to align the organisation's workforce to industry competency models.

Traditionally, in any professional capacity, individuals were referred to as generalists (broad range of skills but may be lacking depth) or specialists (narrow range of in-depth skills but may be lacking wider context). Today's organisations need their workforce to be more diverse, often described as T-shaped, pi-shaped or comb-shaped people.

Table 5: T-, Pi- and Comb-Shaped People

T-shaped	T-shaped individuals are experts in one area, with knowledge of other areas. For example, a developer or tester who also has knowledge of accounting applications.
	T-shaped people tend to be inquisitive; they like to learn new skills and will acquire them as opportunities are made available. Although a clear focus on one competence creates deeper understanding, it can be dangerous to have just one area of profound expertise since the value of any single domain within this self-renewing industry can erode rapidly.
Pi-shaped	A pi-shaped person is strong in two (or more) areas, and knowledgeable in

	others. For example, someone who can both design and develop is desirable for many agile organisations, as well as someone who has good testing skills. In the past, pi-shaped people were often more senior staff, having built up their skills over time working in different domains. That model has changed in the last few years, with new hires arriving at organisations with skills in multiple areas, not yet having specialised in any one specific area.
Comb-shaped	A comb-shaped person has built up multiple specialisms (more than two); for example, someone who has changed career from a business role to an IT role and gained different skills along the way. They are also knowledgeable in other areas. For example, a comb-shaped person might be able to gather requirements and design and develop a product or service, as well as having good knowledge of adjacent areas.

Experience and knowledge come from all aspects of your life. Your family, education, travel, career and hobbies all form part of who you are.

I worked in the past at a UK government department. I was employed by an outsourcing organisation that was taking over management of the department's IT systems. During the transition, I worked with some civil servants who had been part of the organisation for 20 or 30 years. Many of them were incredible specialists. They knew their IT system inside out, and many had been involved in writing or developing the technology they worked with. What we brought was more generalist skill sets. Many of us in the outsourced team had, by the nature of our jobs, worked with multiple organisations and seen many different ways of working. We could combine our skills and our perspective with those of the existing staff to create improvements, based on a combination of generalist and specialist knowledge.

The cautionary note I would add here is to think about your own organisation and make sure it isn't too homogenous. If everyone is a specialist, or everyone is a generalist, you may not have all the competencies you need to deliver services effectively. For example, I have worked with an organisation where everyone on the team was a skilled technical specialist. The organisation was struggling to manage its customer relationships. This was caused by staff being too keen to jump to technical solutions, recommending new software and systems without ever really understanding the problem.

SVS concepts and challenges: Team culture and differences

Culture is made up of values, beliefs, attitudes and behaviours. Culture may be unspoken and unwritten, but it can be observed by looking at how people treat each other and how they work together towards goals in an organisation. Individual teams may have a separate culture, but they will be influenced by the organisational culture.

Successful organisations have a defined culture that is demonstrated in how they work and how their teams perform. Teams should create their operating principles based on the organisation's mission, goals, principles, vision and values. These teams will have a good cultural fit.

Cultural fit defines *"the ability of an employee or team to work comfortably in an environment that corresponds with their own beliefs, values, and needs."*

Successful teams also realise that a high percentage of the problems they will face are based on the relationships between the team members. Therefore, a successful team knows it must manage those relationships for success.

SVS key concepts and challenges: Working to a customer-oriented mindset

A customer-oriented mindset puts the customer at the heart of everything. It cares about customer experience (CX) and makes decisions with customers in mind. It has service empathy. Service empathy defines *"the ability to recognize understand, predict, and project the interests, needs, intentions, and experience of another party, in order to establish, maintain, and improve the service relationship."*

This is supported by the ITIL 4 guiding principle 'focus on value'.

Happy employees are a secret weapon for happy customers. Enthusiastic and engaged employees are your best marketing department. Empowered employees can help customers and deliver a better CX. If employees are happy and have a service- and customer-oriented mindset, they will be much more likely to put customer needs first.

Consider these steps to create a customer-oriented strategy:

- Create a customer value proposition (CVP) – balance benefits and loyalty.
- Map the customer/user experience journey – consider all touchpoints.*
- Recruit customer-friendly staff.
- Treat employees well – happy employees make happy customers.
- Train/coach staff on the customers, products and industries they support.
- Walk the talk. Senior managers should lead by example.
- Listen to the voice of the customer (VoC) – surveys, meetings, etc.
- Use lots of feedback data: consider using a balanced scorecard of metrics.
- Empower staff: give them the authority to solve customer issues.

*A customer journey describes the steps, touchpoints and/or interactions a customer has with an organisation. Customer and user experience includes the customer or user's holistic perception of the journey. If this is relevant to your role or of interest to you in your career development, you can find more information in the *ITIL® 4: Drive Stakeholder Value* publication.

It's easy to say "we are customer-oriented". But is it actually true? I think about my own organisation and how we work with our customers in terms of 'moments of truth'. The Oxford English Dictionary defines a moment of truth as "A time when a person or thing is tested, a decision has to be made, or a crisis has to be faced."

Every interaction with a customer or potential customer can be a moment of truth. I encourage my team to spend time on our website and using our systems every week. I ask them to put themselves in the customer's shoes. How easy is it to find information? How quickly does the helpdesk respond? Is anything out of date or inaccurate?

Some issues can be directly solved by the team members, and others are brought to the team meeting for discussion, prioritisation and resolution.

Some technical teams get lost in their day-to-day work and never actually use the systems they are working on. When did you last log on to your own website, or try to ask a question about your product? The findings from these exercises can be extremely valuable.

SVS concepts and challenges: Employee satisfaction management

If happy employees lead to happy customers, it's important to measure and understand how happy employees are. These measurements can be based on many areas such as culture, climate, activities or overall satisfaction. It's important that the results of any measurement exercise are seen to drive improvements, or there is a risk that employees will stop engaging with the measurement process.

Employee satisfaction can be measured through:

- Surveys – by individual, by team or the whole organisation;
- Formal and/or unstructured meetings;
- One-to-one meetings;
- Reviews of quantitative data, including sickness days or the rate of employee turnover; and
- Morale indicators – such as a happy/sad face button in the canteen.

Some organisations use external companies to run employee surveys. This provides anonymity and can lead to more open feedback. Survey planning needs to consider:

- Survey sponsor and purpose;
- Employees to be surveyed;
- Data collection methods;
- Attributes being measured;

- Start and end dates; and
- How the survey data will be used.

SVS concepts and challenges: Positive communications

Good communication is at the heart of teamwork. It can be particularly challenging in organisations where teams aren't co-located. Communication happens both within and outside the team. Good communication is an important skill for an IT service management professional.

Positive communication is based on the following principles:

- Communication is a two-way process.
- We are all communicating all the time.
- Timing and frequency matter.
- There is no single method of communication that works for everyone.
- The message is in the media.

What does 'good' look like when communicating? Good communication:

- Starts with listening;
- Is efficient, responsive, professional, effective and human-centred;
- Establishes positive relationships;
- Reduces problems and stress;
- Recognises intellectual and emotional needs;
- Promotes trust, empathy and shared goals;
- Identifies issues and improvement opportunities;
- Includes emotional, business and technical responses;
- Is timely, based on appropriately set expectations; and

- Is simple, short, relevant, limited to what is needed and free of jargon.

This is supported by the ITIL 4 guiding principle 'keep it simple and practical'.

In the case study, you learned that the rebrand from HW Banking to Banksbest has created some confusion for customers. Think about a communication plan for Banksbest to help resolve this. What message does Banksbest need to send? When and how? How could this be linked to its strategic goal to be seen as a 'digital first' banking provider?

CHAPTER 2: USING A SHIFT-LEFT APPROACH

What is shift-left?

The idea of 'shift-left' originated in software testing, but its principles can easily apply to other areas in IT or service management. Shift-left means, simply, to move work closer to its source. Moving work closer to the source improves the flow, efficiency and effectiveness of the work. Effective shift-left practices can reduce the overall time for the task.

An easy example of shift-left comes from software development teams. Their normal flow of activity is to gather requirements, design, develop, test and then deliver and support a product or service. With shift-left, the testing activities are moved 'left' – earlier in the cycle – so testing happens much closer to the requirement and design activities. In the software development area, testing was no longer a separate work item, but rather embedded in the earlier activities.

Why is this useful? Some of the benefits include the fact that errors are caught earlier, requirements are clarified and resources are not wasted. Errors caught early in the cycle are much easier and cheaper to fix.

Applying shift-left requires a broad knowledge and skill base. Practitioners (and sometimes users) must be willing to learn the necessary skills and take on tasks. When deploying shift-left techniques, the organisation must understand the difference between the need to pay for additional competencies versus the benefits of shift-left. This is a strategic decision.

Applying shift-left to management

Shift-left practices can be applied to several ITIL practices, including:

- Release management
- Deployment management
- Service validation and testing
- Service request management
- Service desk

The expected outcomes of shift-left are the improvement of work quality, speed and a reduction in the amount of rework required. Shift-left can also reduce the workload/strain on the 'right-side' resource, for example, by reducing the number of support requests that are escalated to second level teams.

Shift-left and other practices

Information security

Shift-left is applicable to activities in the information security management practice. Involving information security management in the work of developers and operational teams (sometimes referred to as DevSecOps) creates the same benefits of shifting testing to the early stages.

For example, a shift-left action could be developing a system with two-factor authentication built in when it goes live, rather than needing to add additional security factors once the system is live.

Change enablement

A key concept in change enablement is the use of a change authority. To achieve the benefits of shift-left for specific change types, why not create a change authority within a development team or the continuous integration and continuous delivery/deployment (CI/CD) pipeline, instead of creating a separate advisory board? Of course, there still needs to be appropriate oversight. For example, automated tests within the CI/CD pipeline could serve as the change authority. As long as the tests are passed, code can be deployed.

Change enablement (referred to as change management in previous versions of ITIL, and in many organisations) is often the cause of arguments between service management teams and development teams working in an agile way. Service management teams see change management as a necessary way to ensure that changes are recorded, assessed, prioritised and implemented in a controlled way. Development teams see change management as an unnecessary layer of bureaucracy that slows down their works and prevents them delivering value.

The truth, in my experience, is somewhere in the middle. The principles of change management are absolutely necessary, but HOW we achieve them can and should evolve over time. ITIL 4 recognises this evolution by adopting the name 'change enablement' to emphasise where the focus of the practice should be.

User support

The activities of traditionally defined first-, second- and third lines of support can apply shift-left, allowing a service desk agent to complete more challenging tasks. In this way, more information and tasks flow to where the event originates, allowing a quicker resolution.

At the user level, self-support portals move the 'answer' closer to the question, freeing up service desk agents to handle more complex questions. Service support portals need to be measured to make sure they are being used and are providing appropriate resolutions. If every user needs to contact the service desk after using the self-support portal, the portal is not fit for purpose.

Building a shift-left approach

There are several steps to consider when building a shift-left approach. These include:

- Identifying shift-left opportunities and goals;
- Cost and benefit clarification (captured in a business case);
- Defining targets;
- Creating the improvement initiative;
- Progress incrementally with feedback using the four dimensions of service management; and
- Reviewing outcomes.

In previous decades, we saw organisations rush to outsource functions, including customer services, human resources and finance. Many of these projects were driven by a desire to save money, and many of them failed for this reason. Because the projects weren't focused on value, the service suffered, and work was brought back in-house.

I've seen similar situations with some organisations that I've worked with, when they look at shift-left and the use of self-service. It can be expensive to run a service desk, so it's tempting to try to identify cost savings. However, the focus here must be on value. Do customers actually want to use a portal, or would they prefer to talk to someone? Does the organisation understand common questions, and is knowledge management effective enough to supply the correct answer at the correct time?

The service desk is often described as the 'shop window' for IT. This can be a dangerous place to try to save money. If the support experience is poor, this can have a significant (and costly) impact on your overall relationship with your customers. I don't mean to say self-service is a bad thing – I remember in my first helpdesk role spending most of my day manually resetting passwords. Giving users the ability to do this themselves was a huge timesaver for both them and me!

Table 6: Building a Shift-left Approach[1]

Step	*Activities*
Identify shift-left opportunities and goals	*Review data from a variety of sources, including:* • *Customer and other stakeholder feedback, on time, cost, or quality metrics* • *Delays in the flow of work due to handovers between teams* • *Project interruptions for repetitive incident support* • *Rework to fix bugs or defects, or other service quality concerns* • *Staff frustration/feedback*
Clarify the costs and benefits of improvement	*Data is needed to support a business case and communicate expectations by, for example:* • *Cost, time, quality, or experience metrics* • *Results from a high-level cost-benefit analysis* • *Identifying affected areas, including practices, processes, people, teams, structures, policies, training,*

---

[1] *ITIL® 4: Create, Deliver and Support*, table 5.1. Copyright © AXELOS Limited 2020. Used under permission of AXELOS Limited. All rights reserved.

	recruitment, roles, and remuneration
Set targets	*Define new targets based on the type of work and the goals. For example:* • *Resolution/fulfilment times* • *Number of escalations/interruptions* • *Number of deployments/day* • *Customer or other stakeholder satisfaction ratings* • *Number of audit failures*
Set up the improvement initiative	*Activities include:* • *Deciding on actions and building them into a coherent strategy* • *Planning the work required* • *Working with key people to sell benefits and impact* • *Communication with employees and stakeholders* • *Establishing rapid feedback channels*
Progress incrementally with feedback	*This step can include any of the four dimensions of service management. For example:* • *Pilot specific tasks to leverage quick wins* • *Periodically analyze quantitative or qualitative feedback, and adjust the shift-left approach*

	• Move a percentage or number of tasks per month *• Benchmark current performance* *• Retrain or redeploy staff* *• Review changing roles and responsibilities* *• Adopt new processes or work instructions* *• Implement or change automation* *• Review and modify contracts with partners and suppliers* *• Update the service catalogue* *• Define new measurements to track benefits*
Review outcomes	*On a periodic basis, or when the initiative ends, it is important to:* *• Identify the achieved benefits, as well as the lessons learned* *• Communicate the achieved benefits to employees, customers, and other stakeholders*

Shift-left benefits

When deployed appropriately, shift-left has many benefits, including:

- Faster resolution times;
- Reduced number of interruptions;
- Reduced cost per incident; and
- Increased task variety for teams.

These benefits cascade to improve customer satisfaction, increase project completion rates, reduce support costs and improve employee satisfaction.

34

CHAPTER 3: PLAN AND MANAGE RESOURCES IN THE SERVICE VALUE SYSTEM

This chapter looks at concepts related to the planning and management of resources in the SVS, including:

- Team collaboration and integration;
- Workforce planning;
- Results-based measurement and reporting; and
- A culture of continual improvement.

Team collaboration and integration

People management is easier when there is a great team culture to support it. Organisations need to honestly identify where their level of teamwork is now, and then identify what areas they might need to change.

To create a great team culture, consider:

- Creating the bigger vision for the team;
- Creating leaders and managers;
- Meeting regularly;
- Integrate socially (within appropriate boundaries);
- Providing feedback;
- Creating and promoting a learning culture;
- Cross-training employees; and
- Encouraging informal teams.

The Banksbest case study hints at some collaboration and integration issues within the organisation – for example the creation of a new digital team, and the 'us and them' attitude between developers and operations. What impact will this have? What might Lucy need to do to ensure poor teamwork doesn't affect her project and deliverables?

Workforce planning

Workforce planning looks after one of the organisation's most important (and expensive) assets. Roles (and their associated knowledge, skills and attitudes) are required to:

- Manage business as usual (BAU);
- Exploit emerging technologies;
- Provide leadership and organisational change; and
- Position the organisation for future strategic plans.

"The purpose of the workforce and talent management practice is to enable organization, leaders, and managers to focus on creating an effective and actionable people strategy (analysing the current workforce, determining future workforce needs, identifying the gap between the present and the future, and implementing solutions) so that the organization can achieve its mission, goals, and strategic objectives."

Workforce and talent management is involved in the whole value chain:

- **Plan:** Understand current and future skills requirements, and staff turnover.
- **Improve:** Continually adapt to meet evolving business needs.
- **Engage:** Understand and forecast changing demand for services and how this will impact the workforce.
- **Design and transition:** Understand competences needed for Agile, DevOps, etc. and define training plans.
- **Obtain/build:** Training, mentoring, succession planning, recruiting or sourcing skills.
- **Deliver and support:** Measure how knowledge, abilities and attitude impact practices.

One change I've noticed recently in some organisations is the move away from the term 'human resources'. These organisations argue that people aren't 'things' or resources to be managed. Phrases like 'workforce' and 'talent management' are becoming more common.

However, changing a word isn't enough on its own. If an organisation stops using the term 'human resources' but still treats employees badly, that's not really a positive step!

Results-based measurement and reporting

To be effective, measurements need to focus on both outputs and outcomes. For many IT departments, this is a change in focus, as traditional IT reporting has been very output-based.

"Outputs are a measure of what your function or organization produced. Output measures are necessary for a function to understand its efficiency, effectiveness, and quality; however, it does not measure the value or impact that your services provide for your customers/consumers. Most process metrics are outputs, as they are one component needed to provide the value that the customer expects. It is the combined outputs of all the processes and activities that create the outcomes."

"The outcome is the level of performance or achievement that the business achieved due to the activities or services your organization provided. Results-based measurements are typically defined as the regular measurement of outcomes and results, which provides information on the effectiveness and efficiency of the services. The inputs to the service included the people, capital, and other assets (customer and service provider) used to conduct the activities that deliver the services.

The purpose of results-based measurements is to understand how well the services are meeting the needs of the customer or is there value in the services provided. There are many quantitative measures provided by operations or administrative groups, typically around the efficiency of the operations or process."

Organisations will measure across the ITIL 4 dimensions:

- Organizations and people
- Information and technology

- Partners and suppliers
- Value streams and processes

When measuring people, measure both behaviours and results. Measure behaviours when:

- There is no strong relationship between behaviours and results;
- Outcomes are far in the future; and
- Results are not in the control of the people being measured.

Measure results when:

- There is a clear link to behaviours
- People have the skills, ability and autonomy to complete work
- People need to feel motivated to deliver results

Organisations measure for many reasons, including:

- To identify their current and planned future state;
- To measure achievement of improvements, changes or plans;
- To measure progress towards goals or objectives;
- To support business decisions;
- To drive behaviours;
- To understand how well services are meeting customer needs/expectations; and
- To identify opportunities for improvement.

This is supported by the ITIL 4 guiding principle 'think and work holistically'.

At Banksbest, Lucy will report back to the CDO after three months of the My Way project. What measures might she use to identify whether or not the project is succeeding?

Culture of continual improvement

ITIL 4 continues to emphasise the importance of a culture of continual improvement. As with previous versions of ITIL, this will include:

- Identifying the right people to drive improvement (and having plans in place in case they leave);
- Leading by example;
- Transparency and trust;
- Celebrating success; and
- Making time for improvement and treating it as part of daily work.

It's such a good idea to have a culture of continual improvement. I absolutely recognise this across my businesses... but I can also tell you just how hard it is to make it stick. We tend to start each calendar year with a planning session in January to give us an overall set of objectives for the year. As part of this, we usually remind ourselves that we need to focus on improvement, and we do really well for the first few months. And then context changes, and the day job takes over, or something we didn't expect happens, and improvement slides down our list of priorities. We have to actively and continually remind ourselves that we need to focus on improvement activities. Eventually, it will become a habit.

CHAPTER 4: THE USE AND VALUE OF TECHNOLOGY ACROSS THE SERVICE VALUE SYSTEM

In this chapter, we'll look at some concepts related to the use and value of information technology across the SVS, including:

- Information models;
- Collaboration and workflow;
- Integration and data sharing;
- Reporting and advanced analytics;
- Integrated service management toolsets;
- Robotic process automation (RPA);
- Artificial intelligence (AI);
- Machine learning (ML); and
- Continuous integration and continuous delivery/deployment.

I have two almost conflicting pieces of advice to start this chapter with.

The first goes back to my early days in service management, when technology was less mature. Service management practitioners emphasised that they were 'technology agnostic', i.e. we defined what needed to be done, and then we didn't care what tool was used to do it. Everything was mapped out before a tool was selected, and there was an emphasis on customisation and forcing requirements onto providers. A lot has changed since then, but the lesson to start with requirements, rather than technology, is still relevant.

At the same time, technology has advanced so much and many tools can unlock new ways of working and thinking. So, for some practices (incident management is a good example), it may be better to start with the tool and use what the manufacturer does to shape how we work. After all, the tool is (hopefully) based on its experience of working with hundreds of customers.

So, what do I mean here? One way to look at it could be that for relatively simple, well understood, repetitive tasks, there's nothing wrong with a technology-led approach. For more complex, less well understood work, it is still worthwhile to spend time thinking about exactly what you want before jumping into the tech.

Information models

As organisations continue to address the digitisation of their products and services, they must also effectively manage the information produced by these digital systems. This information will be held in various systems, which need to be carefully designed, including their key components, terminology and practices for their use. Information must be available to those who need it, and it must be consistent, of good quality and accessible.

Digitisation defines the *"conversion of current products and services to a digital format [so they can be used/processed with technology]."*

Information models allow organisations to develop an understanding of the practices, activities and terminology used within the organisation, as well as a structural model of the key technology and business service components.

Collaboration and workflow

One of ITIL's guiding principles is to 'collaborate and promote visibility'. With a good information model, collaboration becomes more effective. As organisations adopt a more agile business approach, the ability to collaborate across the relevant stakeholders (IT, service consumers, partners, service provider employees, etc.) is crucial. To collaborate successfully, work must be visible, follow a workflow, take place in small topic-specific teams, use simple feedback mechanisms and, most importantly, promote good communication.

I heard someone at a DevOps meetup say that "improving daily work is as important as doing daily work". I couldn't understand this at first. Surely, doing the job is the most important thing? But on reflection, it started to make much more sense and ended in a real 'wow' moment for me. When we think about collaboration and workflow, improvement is more important than doing. Think about

> your own role – how much time do you waste rediscovering information, looking in the wrong place and duplicating investigation that has already been done? I definitely recommend keeping this expression in mind. Information models can help us to understand what we need to improve.

Integration and data sharing

With an information model providing a picture of the technical infrastructure, collaborative teams are ready to address the service design. The outcome of service design activities is a design and deployment plan. Typical service designs will require the integration of multiple systems, with data shared between them. The goal of effective service design is to integrate applications and supporting enterprise systems, linking to the business services.

How is this done? Two technical topologies enable this integration: point-to-point and publish-subscribe.

"Point-to-point integration involves directly linking pairs of systems. This may be suitable for simple services with a small number of integrated systems. There are, however, drawbacks with this approach:

- *The number of connections grows quickly in proportion to the number of integrated systems, requiring $n(n-1)$ integrations to be implemented. A bi-directional integration effectively counts as two separate integrations.*

- *The number of different integration protocols and methods may be high, which increases the complexity."*

"Publish–subscribe is an alternative topology in which messages are published by systems to an event broker, which forwards the message to the systems that have been designated as its recipients. This approach offers better scalability, and the looser coupling reduces the complexity of implementation (the publishing system does not even need to be aware of the subscriber). Reliability, though, may be a challenge, particularly when the publisher is unaware that a subscriber has not received a message.

The broker architecture may be in the form of a bus, in which the transformation and routing is done by adapters local to each integrated system (or hub and spoke), where it is centralized. The bus model is not constrained by the limits of a single hub and as such is more scalable."

Within each design and deployment plan, the service implementation approach must be considered. Depending on the service complexity (such as the number of integrations between systems), ITIL 4 defines three delivery approaches:

- **Big bang**

  "A 'big bang' approach involves the delivery of every integration at once. This has potential benefits for testing because the entire system is in place prior to a live roll-out. However, as with software development, integration projects delivered using this approach can become excessively large and complex, which can lead to issues with, for example, troubleshooting. As a result, the approach is suited to simple service implementations with fewer integrated systems and simpler, lower-risk integration"

- **Incremental**

  "Incremental delivery is a more Agile approach for the integration of multiple components in which new integrations are introduced separately in a pre-defined order. It reduces the scale of each individual delivery into production, thus enabling troubleshooting and resolution of post-deployment issues. This approach can be used in most circumstances. Nevertheless, because the overall service remains incomplete until each integration is in place, service testing may require extensive simulation to account for undelivered elements. There may also be a heavy regression test burden."

- **Direct integration**

  "Direct integration allows individual integrations to be deployed as soon as they are ready, in no predetermined order. This provides greater agility and enables rapid initial progress, as with incremental delivery. The approach may necessitate significant simulation to facilitate adequate testing. Global tests of the entire service, and even of the subsets of functional chains within it, can only be run late in the service implementation."

Infrastructure architects and service designers will create the plans necessary to fulfil service requirements.

Part of the My Way project at Banksbest is My Deposit My Way, which will allow customers to use the camera on their mobile phone to pay in a cheque. Which approach would you recommend using to deliver this functionality?

Reporting and advanced analytics

Once services have been deployed and are being used, data will be captured to manage performance and demonstrate achievement of requirements. Care must be taken when collecting data – the availability of data is vast, so collect wisely.

For data to have value, it must be transformed into meaningful information. Data that has been transformed into useful information not only provides service performance reports but also, through advanced analytics, can help to predict sales, purchasing trends and preferences of customers, or even athletic performance. Data science is the examination of data sets to formulate conclusions. This activity is typically completed by a data engineer.

ITIL defines data as *"information that has been translated into a form that is efficient for movement or processing."* Information is defined as *"data that has been transformed into meaningful insight, statistics, reports, forecasts, and recommendations."*

The use of big data (large volumes of structure, semi-structured, and unstructured data) is commonplace in the business world but also in other areas such as governments, healthcare or research organisations. Big data, characterised by the concepts of volume, velocity and variety, allows the user to understand target markets, trends, customer behaviours and preferences, which allow for more accurate service delivery.

Integrated service management toolsets

To manage the CDS activities, most organisations will use an integrated service management toolset. Its purpose is to automate workflows and provide management information (reports, analytics). The toolset should also support communication requirements and engagement functionalities necessary for the support and delivery of products and services.

An integrated toolset will manage records describing events, requests, changes, agreements, actions and plans, as well as managing information about the infrastructure. This allows the toolset to fully support the activities of the SVS. Work can be managed in real time and the data can be used for analytics and reporting.

Note that an integrated service management toolset supports an information model, integrates data from other enterprise tools and data, performs and/or supports analytics and reporting, and through its workflow functionality, promotes collaboration and communication. However, while the capability of end-to-end value stream integration is possible, it has rarely been exploited. As organisational proficiency in managing an SVS increases, so too will the importance of an integrated service management toolset.

I've worked on multiple projects to select and implement an integrated service management toolset. At the start of my career, there were only a few options available, but now the choices are almost limitless. I'm not going to try to describe the process for choosing the right tool here (it would take too long, and you can find lots of guidance online), but I will mention one area that I've seen become more important as the number of tools available has grown: choosing the right 'size' of tool and supplier for your organisation. If you're a smaller organisation, the best-of-breed tool from the biggest vendor on the market may not be a good fit. Some larger vendors are deliberately choosing to work with larger customers only, as they also recognise the importance of this fit. Choosing the right size of tool and supplier means you'll only pay for the functionality that you need and use, and you can build a better ongoing relationship with your toolset provider.

Robotic process automation

RPA is the use of software robots (bots) that perform manually intensive, repetitive and mundane tasks. These tasks are automated, and the robots tend to simulate humans. RPA is used for high-volume repetitive tasks, like cold calls, data entry and password resets. More advanced applications of RPA can couple ML and AI to react to more complex scenarios.

Consider this example: Remember that last marketing letter you got that was offering additional services? You were to contact "Susan" in the sales department for more information. A phone number and email were provided. Most likely that was an automated task and Susan is a robot. You respond to the marketing letter saying you're not interested in the service described but require additional functionality in the service you already use. That response is now 'read' by Susan and forwarded to the appropriate sales team rather than being discarded.

There are typically three elements to RPA:

- **Process automation**
  "This focuses on automating tasks that depend on structured data (e.g. spreadsheets)"
- **Enhanced and intelligent process automation**
  "This works with unstructured data (e.g. email and documents). This type of automation can learn from experience and applies the knowledge it gathers to other situations."
- **Cognitive platforms**
  "These understand customers' queries and can perform tasks which previously required human intervention."

Benefits from RPA include lower labour costs, increased throughput and increased accuracy. Once deployed, the robots only require software maintenance and service and can work 24/7. As long as the rules the robots follow are accurate, the value proposition increases.

RPA best addresses the 'keep it simple and practical' and 'optimize and automate' principles. Ensure the areas that will use RPA have a process and there is business benefit to deploying RPA. Other guiding principles could be chosen when RPA is being developed – consider the need for collaboration with the business and IT so that the final product meets the business need. Additionally, the 'progress iteratively with feedback' principle is also important as automation is designed and tested.

Artificial intelligence

Above, I mentioned the possibility of coupling AI and ML with RPA. In service management, there is a trend to use AI in process and decision automation (for example, if-then-else decisions within a process flow), conversational interfaces (chatbots), predictive analysis and trend analysis.

A new application of AI has developed for IT operations – AIOps (Artificial Intelligence for IT Operations). Here, big data, analytics and ML are applied to IT operations to detect and predict infrastructure issues, perform proactive performance of system maintenance and tuning, and undertake threshold analysis to understand the 'normal' range of system operation.

AI is one of the most hyped and least understood technology concepts. Users who have seen films about killer machines and are worried about a robot taking their job might be very underwhelmed with their first AI interaction. As with all technologies, we need to understand the fundamental questions before we can implement anything. What are we trying to do? Why? How do we want it to work? I've worked with some organisations that have rushed to implement the AI features in their service management toolset, only to roll them back when they realise they don't have the knowledge management to make AI work effectively. AI is improving all the time and the use cases for its adoption are increasing, but we have a long way to go before we catch up with Hollywood.

Machine learning

ML is an applied form of AI allowing systems to learn and improve without human interaction. Using data, rules and AI, ML systems look for patterns in data and then change the behaviour of the system with the goal of finding the best predictive pattern. Learning occurs using several strategies:

- **Supervised learning**
  Both the starting point and expected output are well defined (data is available for both the input and output). Using mathematical techniques and algorithms, outcomes are predicted, creating a model that can be repeated until a level of accuracy is obtained.

- **Unsupervised learning**
  Algorithms are applied to input data only – data is grouped (clustered) and used in later actions. For example, future behaviour is predicted based on past behaviour (finding a correlation between a cause and effect).

The benefit of ML is its use of data to answer specific questions. ML has the ability to sort through vast amounts of data and make more and more accurate predictions, as long as data is continually fed to the system and the correct algorithms are used. For example, you might want to know who will buy your product. You could input the characteristics of personas who would be interested in your product, as well as characteristics of those who would not buy it. When actual buyer characteristics are introduced, the system adjusts the model of who would or would not purchase the product. As more data is introduced, the system gets smarter and more accurate predictions occur.

Continuous integration and continuous delivery/deployment

Agile practices, specifically software engineering, provide three different methods for the delivery of new or changed software. These methods can also be applied to system development. The methods, collectively known as **CI/CD**, are:

- Continuous integration
- Continuous delivery
- Continuous deployment

Continuous integration

Is defined as *"an approach to integrating, building, and testing code within the software development environment."* As developers store changes in a central source code repository, the application to which the change applies is rebuilt and automated testing takes place. If testing fails, developers can respond quickly. At all times, the software is in a working state. This allows for incremental application improvement.

Continuous delivery

Is defined as *"an approach to software development in which software can be released to production at any time. Frequent deployments are possible, but deployment decisions are taken case by case, usually because organizations prefer a slower rate of deployment."*

Continuous deployment

Is defined as *"an approach to software development in which changes go through the pipeline and are automatically put into the production environment, enabling multiple production deployments per day. Continuous deployment relies on continuous delivery."*

The goal of CI/CD is to deploy smaller changes with higher frequency. This reduces risk (less complexity) and increases the velocity of value delivery (more useful changes delivered more quickly to consumers). In CI/CD, the flow from development to production is optimised, with a focus on removing the bottlenecks that reduce change velocity. Agile and Lean principles provide a foundation for CI/CD activities.

A key element in CI/CD is the pipeline. The flow within the pipeline rests on automation of the build, test and deployment activities. The goal is to remove manual effort (or "toil") from the process, creating efficiencies and cost savings as well as allowing the service to scale more easily as it grows. The term pipeline *"defines the set of tools, integrations, practices, and guardrails which allow a continuous and substantially automated flow of changes, from their initial design and development through to deployment into production."*

It's important to remember that not all situations will benefit from CI/CD. Where requirements are well-defined and/or when an iterative deployment approach creates risk to the organisation, a large-scale planned approach might be a better deployment strategy (in other words, a waterfall approach). CI/CD is better suited to situations where requirements are relatively unknown or where failure doesn't have a high impact and can be managed quickly.

Several ITIL practices will interface with CI/CD activities. Specifically, the practices are:

- Software development and management
- Service validation and testing
- Deployment management
- Infrastructure and platform management
- Release management

CHAPTER 5: VALUE STREAMS FOR NEW SERVICES: REVIEWING SERVICE VALUE CHAINS AND SERVICE VALUE STREAMS

In this chapter and chapters 6–10, we consider:

- How to use a value stream to design, develop and transition new services; and
- How specified ITIL practices contribute to a value stream for a new service.

Several of the ITIL practices are applied to the design, development and transition of a new service. These include:

- Service design;
- Software development and management;
- Deployment management;
- Release management;
- Service validation and testing; and
- Change enablement.

The service value chain is *"an operating model for service providers that covers all the key activities required to effectively manage products and services."*

Let's start with a review of the ITIL 4 service value chain components:

- **Engage**
  "The purpose of engage is to provide a good understanding of stakeholder needs, transparency, and continual engagement and good relationships with all stakeholders."

- **Plan**

  "The purpose of the plan is to ensure a shared understanding of the vision, current status, and improvement direction for all four dimensions and all products and services across the organization."

- **Improve**

  "The purpose of improve is to ensure conditional improvement of product, services, and practices across all value chain activities and the four dimensions of service management."

- **Design and transition**

  "The purpose of design and transition is to ensure that products and services continually meet stakeholder expectations for quality, costs, and time to market."

- **Obtain/build**

  "The purpose of obtain/build is to ensure that service components are available when and where they are needed and meet agreed specifications."

- **Deliver and support**

  "The purpose of deliver and support is to ensure that services are delivered and supported according to agreed specifications and stakeholder's expectations."

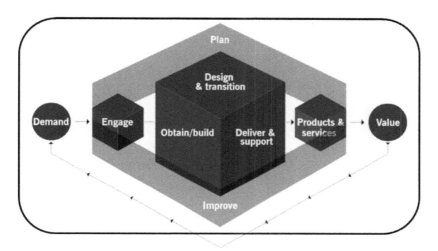

Figure 1: The ITIL service value chain[2]

Using the activities of ITIL's service value chain, it's important to know that every value stream starts with demand and ends with value. A service value stream is "*a series of steps an organization undertakes to create and deliver products and services to consumers.*"

A value stream includes some or all of the ITIL 4 service value chain activities. Activities can happen sequentially or in parallel, or in iterations during an Agile/DevOps style development. Activities can be used multiple times in a single value stream, depending on the situation or scenario. Each step in the value stream can trigger supporting **actions**. Those actions can be fulfilled through the completion of various **tasks**. A value stream can be shown as a series of

---

[2] *ITIL® 4: Create, Deliver and Support*, figure 0.2. Copyright © AXELOS Limited 2020. Used under permission of AXELOS Limited. All rights reserved.

steps touching each value chain activity. Figure 2[3] shows the value streams activity hierarchy.

[3] *ITIL® 4: Create, Deliver and Support*, figure 4.1. Copyright © AXELOS Limited 2020. Used under permission of AXELOS Limited. All rights reserved.

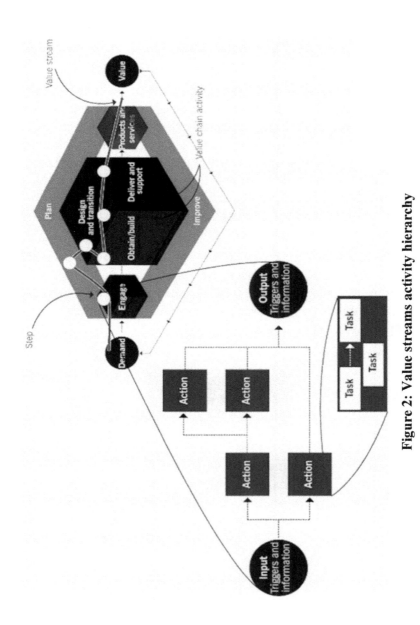

Figure 2: Value streams activity hierarchy

For example, using the above diagram, in the 'engage' activity, a series of actions could be triggered and fulfilled by a series of tasks. The output of those tasks progresses the value stream to the 'plan' activity.

As value streams are defined, remember to visualise them across the organisation. A value stream will represent work across different teams, impacting different stakeholders, using different sets of processes or even different suppliers. Each value stream should clearly indicate touchpoints where users interact with the product, service or supporting staff. Knowing these touchpoints, not only with the user but with other stakeholders, can indicate potential points of failure or the connection of value to demand.

Don't forget, in ITIL terms, an organisation *"can be a single person (e.g., a self-employed programmer or consultant), a team (e.g., a development or support team acting as a business unit), an enterprise, or even an ecosystem of enterprises working together."*

Why not try mapping out a value stream for an activity that you're involved with? You can choose something from your professional or personal life. Do you see any opportunities for improvement?

Creating a value stream

When creating a value stream, consider these general elements:

- Perspective – does the value stream reflect how the service provider wants things to be (their aspirations) or does it reflect how work is actually being done?
- Start with demand and end with value – focus on the entire customer journey, taking an 'outside-in'* approach, and involving all stakeholders as early as possible.
- Consider flexibility and granularity – the value stream should reflect practices with the ability to add a step or iterate steps as needed.
- Management of the steps – clearly define what each step is, its location in the value chain activities and the order of completion; if an action and its tasks span multiple value chain activities, break down the action to reflect this.
- Add processes or procedures from the ITIL practices where applicable.

* Outside-in thinking focuses on the customer's experience and desires. Inside-out thinking (often based on the IT/service provider perspective) focuses on what the organisation wants and may be based on assumptions about what the customer wants.

There are five steps to follow when designing a value stream:

1. Define the use case (how a user uses a system to accomplish a specific goal) or scenario for the value stream.
   a. *"Consider the demand for the value stream*
   b. *The triggers created by the demand*
   c. *The outcomes of the value stream*
   d. *Value created or restored"*
2. Document the steps required to move through the service value chain from demand to value.
3. Map the steps to the service value chain activities.
4. Fragment the steps into actions and tasks, as necessary.
5. Identify practices and resources that will help complete each step/action/task considering the four dimensions.

It is important to create a value stream collaboratively. A series of meetings or workshops is ideal to help develop a clear understanding of needs and outcomes. Optimise the value stream by looking for opportunities to automate, bottlenecks that need to be eliminated, and areas where feedback loops can improve the quality of the output.

Value stream steps

What information should be captured to describe a value stream step? Consider these elements:

- **Input trigger**
  What action will start the step?
- **Information**
  What information is necessary to create the defined outputs/outcomes? When is the information available?
- **Practices**

Tools, technologies, individuals and other resources from the organisation's practices that will assist in completion of the step.

- **Actions/Tasks**

  What needs to happen to achieve the required output? Can the task be completed in parallel? Do they have prerequisites? How long will each task take?

- **Constraints**

  Are there any compliance or policy requirements?

- **Outputs**

  What should be provided by the task? (The value created by the step.)

- **Lead time**

  How much time is necessary to complete the step including any wait time?

Metrics for a value stream

Once we think of a value stream as an expanded workflow, it can be measured via common workflow metrics. You can see these in the diagram below and then the definition of each of the measures.

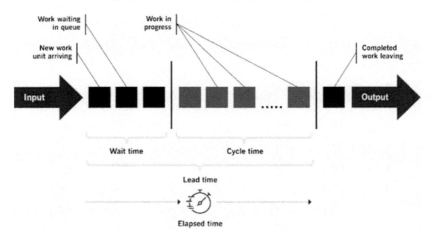

Figure 3: Process timing[4]

- **Cycle time**
  Amount of time to complete a discrete unit of work.
- **Wait time**
  Amount of time a discrete unit of work waits in a queue.
- **Lead time**
  Sum of cycle and wait times (total time to complete a discrete unit of work).
- **Process queue**
  Number of discrete units of work waiting to be processed.
- **Work in progress (WIP)**

---

[4] *ITIL® 4: Create, Deliver and Support*, figure 4.2. Copyright © AXELOS Limited 2020. Used under permission of AXELOS Limited. All rights reserved.

Number of discrete units being processed but not yet completed.

- **Throughput**
  Number of discrete units of work processed per time unit.

Value stream for a new service

Product and service development can use an Agile or a waterfall approach. Agile software development allows requirements and solutions to evolve through iterative and incremental practices. Waterfall development is more linear, with each task relying on deliverables from the previous stage.

There are several ITIL 4 practices that may contribute to the creation of value streams for new services. Please note that not all the practices listed here are examinable as part of the ITIL 4 Specialist Create, Deliver and Support syllabus. The practices in bold are examinable.

- Portfolio management
- Business analysis
- Risk management
- Financial management
- Architecture management
- **Service design**
- Capacity and performance management
- Availability management
- Information security management
- Service continuity management
- Supplier management

- Project management
- **Software development and management**
- Infrastructure and platform management
- Service level management
- **Service validation and testing**
- **Deployment management**
- **Release management**
- **Change enablement**

CHAPTER 6: ITIL PRACTICES AND VALUE STREAMS FOR NEW SERVICES

In this chapter, we introduce the links between the ITIL 4 practices and value streams for new services. We will then move on to study some of ITIL practices in detail in the following chapters. The relevant practices are:

- Change enablement
- Service design
- Software development and management
- Service validation and testing
- Release management
- Deployment management

Scenario for a new service

We can use the Banksbest case study to consider how the six examinable practices would be used in developing and deploying the new My Way service. The project has been approved and will be funded via the digital transformation budget. The initial deployment will follow an Agile way of working (using incremental development and delivery).

- **Demand:** strategic decision to expand the company portfolio with new ways to access services, market analysis of customer preferences.
- **Engage:** acknowledgement and documentation of demand – develop business case-like information (benefits, costs, risks).

- **Plan:** ensure the new service fulfils the strategic direction of Banksbest and can be met through the use of current technology, staff capabilities, partner agreements and in-place processes.
- **Design and transition:** Agile methods; increase business, technical, and service capacity; plan release/deployment.
- **Obtain/build:** have necessary service components (technical and non-technical) available when needed.
- **Deliver and support:** Implement the release plan; availability of functionality, trained staff.
- **Improve:** update functionality based on feedback; improve online interaction processes, possibly via a concierge service; define needed processes before automation.
- **Value:** increased range of services available to customers, position in business banking vertical).

Banksbest will use the portfolio management and business analysis practices to make the decision to pursue the My Way project. These two practices assess the current strategy (business analysis) and compare to their current investments (portfolio management). Once approved, requirements are gathered to meet the desired outcomes for the project (business analysis).

As this project has been approved, change enablement engages to ensure that changes to the services and their components are controlled, authorised and risk mitigated. The risk management practice may also play a role here. Control ensures that no change is deployed without authorisation and each change has fulfilled the practice requirements. Authorisation means that every change within the practice scope will be reviewed and approved as per the practice requirements. Risk mitigation ensures that every change will be assessed for risk (to the infrastructure, to the organisation, etc.) and controls will be put in place to mitigate the potential risk.

Central to the change enablement practice is the ability to balance effectiveness, throughput, compliance and risk control for the changes within its scope. Balancing these four factors allows the practice to work well with Agile development methods (e.g. smaller, more frequent changes typically have decreased risk, are easier to deploy and have less impact on the system).

Changes are submitted to initiate the activities within service design and software development and management. These two practices will collaborate to create the overall design of the My Way service and the specific design for the necessary infrastructure changes. Service design will identify the design model(s), the necessary resources, and plans for the new service, ensuring utility and warranty. Improvement activities for both the service and the service design practice are included in the overall design.

Software development and management will follow Agile practices and refine the requirements using user stories and then proceed to development of multiple iterations of functionality based on the criticality of each requirement. Each iteration of development will be assessed against current infrastructure capabilities to create:

- The technical requirements for the My Way application suite;
- Testing plans;

- User documentation;
- Actual code;
- Infrastructure configuration plans; and
- Any other plans necessary.

As Agile practices are being followed, the service validation and testing practice will engage simultaneously with the service design and software development and management practices. Tests, defined in the design, will be executed to ensure the new service meets the defined requirements. Test plans are used (and reused) to reduce the risks and uncertainties that the new service will potentially introduce into the live environment.

Service validation and testing uses reusable test models based on the testing strategy and test standards. The result of the testing is to confirm the achievement of the requirements as well as to mitigate the risk associated with deploying a new change to the infrastructure.

The last two practices address the planning of a release and then the actual deployment of the new service. Release management defines the various release models, plans and schedule. A review process of the release management activities looks to improve the activities of release as well as the release practice itself. Deployment management takes the approved, tested, risk-reduced release and moves it into the production/live environment. Each deployment will follow a defined deployment model (continues the release model; both practices could be combined to create a single practice) to ensure the planned, developed, tested and authorised change is transitioned to the live environment as intended, meeting the agreed requirements.

After reading this section, why not try to apply the practices to a new product or service that you've been involved with? Does the exercise highlight any areas for improvement?

Using the ITIL 4 practice guides

A practice is *"a set of organizational resources designed for performing work or accomplishing an objective. These resources are grouped into the four dimensions of service management."*

The practice guides are hosted on the *My ITIL* site.[5] Anyone who takes an ITIL exam will have one year's access to My ITIL, or there are paid subscriptions available. This publication contains all the material you need to pass the exam, but if you wish to access the practice guides for further reading during or after your studies, you will need to use the My ITIL site.

The practice guides are used to describe the 34 ITIL 4 practices and are referred to in all Specialist, Strategist and Leader publications. Additionally, selected content in the guides will contribute to the syllabuses for these courses.

ITIL Foundation: ITIL 4 Edition provides a brief overview of each practice. The other four publications (CDS, DPI,

---

[5] *www.axelos.com/my-axelos/my-itil*.

HVIT, DSV) all refer to the guides and describe how they can be applied.

CHAPTER 7: VALUE STREAMS FOR NEW SERVICES: CHANGE ENABLEMENT

This chapter looks at some of the details around the change enablement practice. This includes:

- Purpose and description;
- Complexity-based approach to changes;
- Practice success factors; and
- Roles: change manager, change coordinator and change authority.

Purpose and description

A change is *"the addition, modification, or removal of anything that could have a direct or indirect effect on services."*

Change enablement has a purpose of *"maximizing the number of successful service and project changes by ensuring that risks have been properly assessed, authorizing changes to proceed, and managing the change schedule."*

Change is constant but needs to be controlled so that it meets the needs and expectations of those affected. Changes that are authorised (meaning they have been planned, reviewed, tested and risk-mitigated) should enable the desired outcomes.

Today's digital organisation requires flexibility and agility, and the change enablement practice embraces these characteristics through three intents:

- *"Changes are planned and realized in the context of value streams*
- *The practice does not aim to unify all the changes planned and carried out in an organization*
- *The focus of the practice is on balancing effectiveness, throughput, compliance, and risk control for all changes in the defined scope."*

Complexity-based approach to changes

Balancing change effectiveness, throughput and risk control requires careful planning in terms of authorisation and overall control. What safeguards are needed for each situation? Consider the continuum shown in the diagram below: some changes are relatively predictable with little or no risk, while others are more volatile with an unknown risk impact. Figure 4[6] shows what changes are needed in all business situations.

---

[6] *ITIL® 4: Practice Guide: Change Enablement*, figure 2.1. Copyright © AXELOS Limited 2020. Used under permission of AXELOS Limited. All rights reserved.

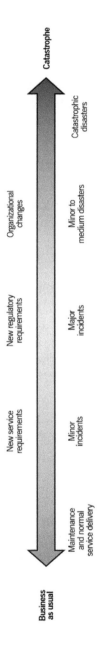

Figure 4: Changes are needed in all business situations

Changes that have a well-understood outcome can be standardised and perhaps automated. This will decrease change costs and reduce the time taken to deliver the change. Consider the use of checklists and templates with these types of changes. Examples of standard changes include routine infrastructure maintenance, fulfilling a service request, and routine software updates.

ITIL 4 defines a standard change as *"a low-risk, pre-authorized change that is well understood and fully documented, and which can be implemented without needing additional authorization."*

Changes that have greater complexity and less predictability require a process where there is expert assessment, authorisation and control. These changes are classified as 'normal' changes. Normal changes have a varying level of risk associated with them. Because these changes require authorisation, there needs to be an appropriate change authority associated with each of them. A change authority can be a person or a group with the responsibility for authorising a change.

Low-risk changes require an authority that can make rapid decisions. Often, automation is used to speed up the change. High-risk changes will require additional authority before they can progress; that change authority might be a management board.

A common trigger for change is the change request, which creates a record of the change showing actions and expected outcomes of the various actions to complete the change. Organisations that follow CI/CD practices will have automated most of the change enablement process. Another method to handle changes consistently and quickly is through the use of change models. Change models provide a repeatable approach for a type of change, allowing the change to be carried out in a consistent way. Procedures and rules have been predetermined to address the assessment, authorisation and control of changes. Apply the four dimensions to the change model to ensure a comprehensive view.

But what about emergencies? In an emergency situation, changes still need to be deployed effectively, safely and promptly. An emergency change is a type of change used when a 'fix' is needed as soon as possible. An emergency change model may bypass some procedures (for example, registering a change request, or fully testing the change) and may also have a dedicated change authority who has sufficient authority and availability to hold that role.

Two considerations for emergency changes are:

- There are still rules and controls; and
- Testing may be bypassed if the situation warrants it (e.g. the cost of the delay is equal or higher than the risks associated with an unsuccessful change).

Emergency changes should be reviewed after they have taken place, and the appropriate documentation should be completed. If an organisation experiences a high level of emergency changes, this may be an indication that the change enablement practice is ineffective.

I've worked as both a change analyst and a change manager. My change manager role was more than ten years ago, before DevOps, CI/CD, Agile, etc. were common terms in the IT department. Change management was carried out using a change advisory board (CAB), with attendees from the client and the outsourced IT provider and with technical and service-related roles attending. Much of the work we did manually at that meeting can now be automated – testing, backout plans, performance, etc. One element that can't be automated is the relationships the CAB built. The discussions in the CAB meetings were sometimes heated when different priorities clashed, but they always added value by highlighting problems and allowing us to discuss them, human to human. The respect that we built in the CAB improved how we worked together outside of the meeting and helped to create bridges between teams; the importance of this must be recognised. Make sure you don't lose the human element in a rush to automate interactions.

Practice success factors

A practice success factor (PSF) is *"a complex functional component of a practice that is required for the practice to fulfil its purpose."*

PSFs for change enablement include components from the four dimensions. The activities and resources used within each PSF ensure the practice is effective.

There are four PSFs defined for the change enablement practice:

- *"Ensuring that changes are realized in a timely and effective manner;*
- *Minimizing the negative impacts of changes;*
- *Ensuring stakeholder satisfaction with changes and change enablement;*
- *Meeting change-related governance and compliance requirements."*

Changes are realised in a timely manner

The focus of change enablement is effective and timely change – you will notice that this has both an output and an outcome focus. It is important to understand both perspectives – they are equally important and should be measured by change enablement.

The output focus defines *"a change that has successfully transformed from its initial state to the pre-designed target state."* The outcome focus defines *"a change that has successfully contributed to the achievement of the desired pre-defined outcomes."*

To improve the effectiveness and timeliness of changes, consider the following areas:

- Decrease the size of individual changes (decompose large changes into a series of smaller changes).
- Standardise and automate where possible.

- Ensure there is a feedback loop for each iteration of change planning and realisation.
- Good requirements gathering – understand expectations and use good communication.
- Ensure integration with other ITIL practices for effective change to value streams.

Minimise any negative impact

Changes are a common source for service disruption and have the potential to create risk. The change enablement practice describes processes and activities to mitigate or eliminate disruption and/or risk. To ensure that changes are effective, timely, and risk-mitigated, consider these areas:

- Use change models.
- Automate standardised changes.
- Work to reduce change sizes.
- Assess the impact of changes to the infrastructure, services and stakeholders.

Ensure stakeholder satisfaction

The change enablement practice ensures stakeholders are identified and their expectations are documented, considered and addressed, as needed. Other practices, such as business analysis, risk management and relationship management, assist in these activities. Change enablement will continually monitor stakeholder engagement and satisfaction during change realisation and once the change has been completed. Data that is used to manage satisfaction is good communication, status updates and collecting (and acting upon) feedback.

Using the Banksbest case study, identify stakeholders for 'My Deposit My Way'. What criteria could be used to measure satisfaction for each stakeholder type? What would Doug's role as a stakeholder be?

Meet governance and compliance requirements

Governance and compliance requirements have a direct impact on change. Change enablement ensures these requirements are understood, and that they are met within each change. Compliance and governance requirements are met through:

- The use of controls in change models, processes and procedures;
- The provision of required information; and
- The initiation of improvement activities to prevent or correct non-compliance.

Roles

The change enablement practice explicitly defines three roles:

- Change manager
- Change coordinator
- Change authority

The responsibilities for the change manager include:

- Initial review and verification of change requests;
- Assignment of changes to teams for assessment and authorisation as defined by change models;
- Communication;
- Monitoring and reviewing teams that build and test changes;
- Publishing the change schedule;
- Carrying out analysis; and
- Initiating improvements across all aspects of the practice (models, processes, activities, etc.).

The change manager and the change coordinator have similar responsibilities – they differ only in scope. The scope is much more limited for the coordinator and would entail a specific type of change, geographic location or division of an organisation.

Traditionally, a CAB was established as the change authority to review and authorise changes. In some organisations, they became bottlenecks, introducing delays and limiting the throughput of changes.

Changes should be authorised based on considerations including resource, cost and priority. This type of assessment can be built into change model activities by defining the requirements and procedure for authorisation.

Delegate the change authority responsibility to an appropriate level such as a service owner, technical expert or development team. Assessment and authorisation can be manual, automated or skipped for specific types of change.

ITIL 4 defines the change authority as a *"role responsible for the assessment and authorization of a change during its lifecycle (from initiation to completion)."*

Change enablement key takeaways

Two key takeaways should be recognised for the change enablement practice:

- Standardisation and automation can be hugely beneficial as they significantly accelerate change while maintaining control.
- Decreasing the size of changes can increase the effectiveness and throughput of the practice while decreasing the level of risk.

Think about how change is managed in your own organisation. Are changes typically successful? What processes and procedures are followed? Where do you see the potential for improvement based on the content in this chapter?

CHAPTER 8: VALUE STREAMS FOR NEW SERVICES: SERVICE DESIGN AND SOFTWARE DEVELOPMENT AND MANAGEMENT

This chapter looks at the service design practice and the software development and management practice. Specific areas of interest include:

- Purpose and description;
- Design thinking (service design concept);
- Scope of software development and management; and
- Practice success factors.

Purpose and description

To understand these two practices and how they interrelate, we should consider the purpose statements for each of them.

The purpose of the service design practice is *"to design products and services that are fit for purpose and use, and that can be delivered by the organization and its ecosystem. This includes planning and organizing people, partners and suppliers, information, communication, technology, and practices for new or changed products and services, and the interaction between the organization and its customers."*

The purpose of software development and management is *"to ensure that applications meet internal and external stakeholder needs, in terms of functionality, reliability, maintainability, compliance, and auditability."*

When comparing the two purpose statements, it's clear that service design ensures products and services fulfil their utility and warranty requirements, while software development and management focuses on the development and management of application software to meet utility and warranty needs.

As we explore other aspects of service design, the activities clearly focus on identifying tasks, defining key information and coordinating the implementation. This practice is very much managerial, and it oversees the entire lifecycle of a service design. Software development and management would naturally coordinate with service design to ensure a smooth transition of any developed applications to support the new product or service.

There are unique elements to each practice that allow the practice to meet its purpose.

Design thinking

One concept unique to service design is design thinking.

"Design thinking is a practical and human-centered approach that accelerates innovation. It is used by product and service designers as well as organizations to solve complex problems and find practical, creative solutions that meet the needs of the organization and its customers."

Design thinking is complementary to Lean and Agile methodologies as it is iterative and applied by multidisciplinary teams. Design thinking activities include:

- **Inspiration and empathy** – developed by watching people interact with products and services and identifying how that reaction changes with a different solution.

- **Ideation** – combines divergent (offers multiple unique ideas) and convergent (the ability to find a preferred solution) thinking.
- **Prototyping** – tests the ideation results through iteration and refinement, allowing innovation to speed up as well as learning strengths and weaknesses of new solutions.
- **Implementation** – where the solution becomes alive via coordination with other service management practices. This can follow Agile principles (iterative deployment).
- **Evaluation** – measures the actual performance of the preferred solution, ensures acceptance criteria are met and documents any improvement opportunities.

Good design can be almost invisible. Bad design can confound and frustrate your users with each product or service interaction. Effective service design practices build strong relationships with service users. Poor design is expensive to fix (in time and resources) and can also lead to costs in terms of missed opportunities.

One organisation I worked with had a 'pet' project that had been approved by a senior person in the IT department. The project goal was to create a notification screen that would appear on every user's computer when they started work, to let them know about any company information or changes. The project was already over time and over budget, but the sponsor was suffering from the sunk cost fallacy – so much money had been spent, that they couldn't bring themselves to stop the work.

When the project eventually went live, user feedback was terrible. The users found the notifications intrusive and distracting. After a short time, it was quietly shut down.

With better service design, this project could have been a success – or could have been stopped much earlier. It's always dangerous to assume that we know what is best for our users, and the ITIL 4 concept of value co-creation is key here.

The scope of software development and management

As one would expect, the scope of software development and management is specific to applications (software). The activities of this practice focus exclusively on application development, software and software artefact management, and the operation of the application. The resources used by software development and management are application artefacts, including the specification, resultant designs, source code, object code and supporting documentation.

Software development and management responsibilities include:

- Application owners, who provide requirements; and
- Infrastructure management, which provides the environments for development and management activities, and the production environment operation.

Practice success factors

Service design has two PSFs:

- Ensure the approach to service design is organisation-wide.
- Ensure services fulfil utility and warranty requirements throughout their lifecycle.

In the Banksbest case study, do you notice any information that might suggest Banksbest will find it hard to take an organisation-wide approach to service design? What could it do to make sure it achieves this?

Software development and management also has two PSFs:

- Agree and improve an organisational approach to software development and management.
- Ensure that software meets the defined requirement and quality criteria.

Both practices focus on an organisation-wide application of their practice activities. Both also focus on the quality and value of the practice outcomes. What should be noted is the concept of models in these two practices – both advocate that there can be several models or approaches to accommodate the different types of products and services. The approach used will depend on the customer requirements and organisational objectives.

CHAPTER 9: VALUES STREAMS FOR NEW SERVICES: SERVICE VALIDATION AND TESTING

This chapter looks at elements of the service validation and testing practice. Specific elements are:

- Purpose and description;
- Scope; and
- Practice success factors.

Purpose and description

The purpose of service validation and testing is "*to ensure that new or changed products and services meet defined requirements.*"

As a reminder, "*the definition of service value is based on input from customers, business objectives, and regulatory requirements and is documented as part of the design and transition value chain activity. These inputs are used to establish measurable quality and performance indicators that support the definition of assurance criteria and testing requirements.*"

The activities of service validation and testing aim to reduce the introduction of risks and uncertainties into the live environment as new or changed products and services are deployed. The practice needs to recognise that testing every possibility is usually impossible due to cost and time constraints. The level of testing needs to be clearly defined, based on:

- "*Agreed requirements that a service or product must meet*"

- *"Impact and likelihood of deviations from the agreed requirements"*

Understanding the requirements with respect to the possible deviations allows for informed testing (allowing the organisation to test the areas where the deviations are most likely).

Service validation takes place early in the lifecycle (during ideation and design) and its purpose is to confirm the design will meet the agreed requirements. Service validation also establishes acceptance criteria for the next stages (development, deployment and release).

Testing is based on the criteria developed during the validation activities. Test strategies and test plans are developed and implemented. Test plans are based on test strategies.

A test strategy *"defines an overall approach to testing and can be applied to environments, platforms, sets of services or individual products or services."* Test plans *"define the detailed activities, estimates, and schedules for each test phase (levels of testing)."*

Today's digital environment requires velocity, security, agility and stability. Service validation and testing need to reflect those characteristics. This is achieved through a close integration with the following practices:

- Architecture management
- Software development and management
- Project management
- Infrastructure and platform management
- Release management

- Deployment management
- Incident management
- Problem management

Don't forget the different roles and their collaborative work: testers, developers and operations teams need to work together to formulate the appropriate tests and correctly interpret results.

It surprises me that I still see organisations that treat testing as a silo, cut off from all other design and development activities. Many organisations still take a waterfall approach to testing, adding it at the end of the project timeline. This means that they miss early opportunities for improvement; it can also lead to testing activities being compressed or even skipped altogether when project deadlines are overrun. Consider how testing takes place in your organisation, and whether there are opportunities to improve through concepts like shift-left and test-driven development (TDD). Testing should be a thread that runs through the entire product or service lifecycle.

Scope

The scope of service validation and testing includes:

- Translating the requirements for products or services into deployment and release management acceptance criteria;
- Establishing test approaches and defining test plans for new or changed products and services;
- Eliminating risk and uncertainty of new or changed products and services by testing;
- Discovering new information about new or changed products and services by testing; and
- Continually reviewing test approaches and methods to improve the efficiency of the tests.

There are other practices that include activities and responsibilities that relate to service validation and testing. These practices are listed in the following table:

Table 7: Activities Related to the Service Validation and Testing Practice Described in Other Practice Guides[7]

Activity	*Practice Guide*
Establishing detailed requirements for the utility and warranty of the new or changed product or service	*Business analysis*
Analyzing new requirements for services	

---

[7] *ITIL® 4: Practice Guide: Service Validation and Testing*, table 2.2. Copyright © AXELOS Limited 2020. Used under permission of AXELOS Limited. All rights reserved.

outside of existing utility and warranty options	
Maintaining financial control over testing *Defining a testing budget*	*Financial management*
Developing and managing software	*Software development and management*
Developing and managing infrastructure	*Infrastructure and platform management*
Operational communications with users and feedback gathering	*Service desk*
Deploying services and components	*Deployment management*
Releasing services	*Release management*
Ongoing management and implementation of improvements	*Continual improvement*
Establishing detailed requirements for the utility and warranty of the new or changed product or service	*Business analysis*

Analyzing new requirements for services outside of existing utility and warranty options	

Practice success factors

There are two PSFs for service validation and testing:

- *"Defining and agreeing an approach to the validation and testing of the organization's products, services, and components in line with the organization's requirements for speed and quality of service changes.*
- *Ensuring that new and changed components, products, and services meet agreed criteria"*

Define and agree an approach to validation and testing

Based on the first PSF, service validation and testing should develop an approach to capture the utility and warranty requirements for any product, service or component. They will gather this information from:

- Stakeholders (customer and user requirements and feedback);
- Business requirements;
- Compliance and regulatory requirements; and
- Security and risk controls.

These requirements should then be translated into acceptance criteria for the product or service.

Ensuring new and changed components, products and services meet agreed criteria

"*Ensuring that new and changed components, products, and services meet agreed criteria*" is the second PSF for service validation and testing. To achieve this outcome, the test strategy is critical. A test strategy is created for each project and is tailored to the project outcomes.

Testing elements

There are several elements that should be defined and managed when considering the test strategy. They include:

- *"Test organization – separate testers from developers to remove bias*
- *Test planning and control – match testing methodology with the development methodology (e.g., involve testing in each iteration or increment if following an Agile approach), the type of system/service (e.g., testing a financial system where the system has different requirements throughout year when compared to an online shopping site), and fully considering the activities around the application elements (e.g., consider data migration, training, operational readiness, release management practices, reporting, etc.).*
- *Test analysis and design – report on the progress of testing with a full understanding of the test schedule (what has been done and what remains) before drawing any conclusions of success or failure of the test results*

9: Values streams for new services: Service validation and testing

- *Phases and cycles – consider the order of tests when planning (e.g., test the new features first as they tend to have the highest risk of negative impact)*
- *Test preparation and execution – provision the test environment carefully and protect the test data so when the tests are executed, the results are indicative of the prepared environment and no other factors*
- *Evaluating exit criteria and reporting – know when to stop! Previously defined acceptance (exit) criteria define 'good enough' and testing stops at this point. Tests that have failed, should be report and correction action taken*
- *Test closure – can trigger early life support (ELS) activities, release of test resources, archiving test assets (strategies, plans, reports, scripts), capture lessons learned for continual improvement."*

The ITIL 4 guidance mentions separating test roles from development roles to reduce bias. Often referred to as segregation or separation of duties, this is a traditional approach that is meant to stop people 'checking their own homework'. A developer might deliberately let a failed test pass to save time, or they might accidentally let an error through because their familiarity with the product prevents them from recognising it. Roles were also separated so that audit or governance requirements could be met.

However, approaches like TDD rely on developers writing their own tests before creating the code to pass the test. Highly regulated organisations that have adopted Agile development methods have found ways to meet their regulatory requirements.

It's good practice to ensure no one is put into a position where they feel compelled to make a bad decision, but strict separation of development and test roles is no longer necessary.

CHAPTER 10: VALUE STREAMS FOR NEW SERVICES: RELEASE MANAGEMENT AND DEPLOYMENT MANAGEMENT

This chapter looks at two closely related practices: release management and deployment management. We will explore the following areas:

- Purpose and description.
- Scope.
- Practice success factors.

Purpose and description

"The purpose of the release management practice is to make new and changed services and features available for use."

"The purpose of the deployment management practice is to move new or changed hardware, software, documentation, processes, or any other component to live environments. It may also be involved in deploying components to other environments for testing or staging."

Simply put, release ensures services are available for use, and deployment performs the actual task of moving the 'release' to a designated environment.

A release is defined as *"a version of a service or any other configuration item, or a collection of configuration items that is made available for use."*

Release management scope

Release management has a very simple scope:

10: Value streams for new services: Release management and deployment management

- *"Develop and maintain the organizational approach to release new and changed services and components*
- *Manage and coordinate all release instances in line with the defined approach, from planning, to implementation, and review."*

Release management must also plan for the removal of services and components where necessary (this is referenced in the 'new and changed' phrase).

Deployment management scope

The scope of deployment management revolves around the successful transition (add, move, modify, remove) of products and services. Deployments are authorised by change enablement. Specifically, the scope states:

- *"The effective transition of products, services, and service components between controlled environments, such as the development, live, test, and staging environments.*
- *The effective removal of products, services, and service components from designated environments."*

Release management practice success factors

The PSFs for release management focus on:

- Developing a consistent approach to the release of products and services; and
- Ensuring the release of products and services effectively integrate with the organisational value streams and service relationships.

10: Value streams for new services: Release management and deployment management

The use of release models ensures consistency in the release activities. Flexibility is needed in the creation of a model to ensure it can be adapted to changing circumstances such as scale, urgency and complexity. A continual improvement approach should be followed to eliminate waste and ensure effectiveness.

A release model will reflect an agreed approach to the release management activities for a specific product. The model will include several aspects, including:

- An agreed high-level approach;
- Target user audience of the release(s);
- Rules for user enablement;
- Release units and packaging rules;
- Push/pull conditions;
- Verification and acceptance criteria; and
- Terms and conditions of release usage.

There will be multiple release models to support the services delivered. There could also be more than one release model for the same product, which is dependent on the market or consumers of that service.

To ensure that the release of new products and services effectively supports the value stream, consider the impact of elements from all four service management dimensions. Additionally, as release models are developed and deployed, coordination, automation and good planning are required for a successful release. Practices that coordinate with release management are software deployment and management, infrastructure and platform management, deployment management, service validation and testing, and release management.

Review the following table for other practices that describe activities from release management within their practice activities.

Table 8: Release Management[8]

Activity	*Practice Guide*
Authorization of changes/releases	*Change enablement*
Deployment of new and changed components and services in live environment	*Deployment management*
Development of software	*Software development and management*
Development and building of infrastructure components	*Infrastructure and platform management*
User training *Support and operational staff training*	*Workforce and talent management*
Testing and validating the services and service components	*Service validation and testing*

[8] *ITIL® 4 Practice Guide: Release Management*, table 2.1. Copyright © AXELOS Limited 2020. Used under permission of AXELOS Limited. All rights reserved.

Naming, versioning and control of the service components	Service configuration management
Management of organizational changes related to large-scale releases	Organizational change management
Management of projects	Project management

Deployment management practice success factors

The two PSFs for deployment management mirror the PSFs for release management:

- Developing a consistent approach to the deployment of products and services.
- Ensuring the release of products and services effectively integrates with the organisational value streams.

The use of deployment models ensures consistency in the deployment activities. Deployment models are based on several factors, including automation, frequency, rate of change, source of components and visibility of the change. Each deployment model should also define the flow of activity through the target environment, roles and responsibilities, triggers, and interfaces with other practices.

To ensure effective deployments, changes and releases must be strictly managed. Component integrity is crucial – there should be no unauthorised activity to the change or release during the deployment activities. The effectiveness and efficiency of a deployment depends on the availability of resources, skills, technology, tools and infrastructure. The use of automation improves the deployment practice through better consistency, removal of manual error, and efficiency.

Review the following table for other practices that describe activities from deployment management within their practice activities.

Table 9: Deployment Management[9]

Activity	*Practice Guide*
Authorizing changes/releases	*Change enablement*
Making services and components in the live environment available to users	*Release management*
Developing software	*Software development and management*
Developing and building infrastructure components *Preparing and maintaining target environments for deployments*	*Infrastructure and platform management*

---

[9] *ITIL® 4 Practice Guide: Deployment Management*, table 2.2. Copyright © AXELOS Limited 2020. Used under permission of AXELOS Limited. All rights reserved.

10: Value streams for new services: Release management and deployment management

Providing IT assets to be deployed *Maintaining authorized repositories of service components*	*IT asset management*
Testing and validating services and service components	*Service validation and testing*
Naming, versioning, and controlling the service components	*Service configuration management*

CHAPTER 11: VALUE STREAMS FOR USER SUPPORT

Value stream mapping can be used to improve existing value chains. In this chapter, our focus is on user support. Most organisations will have a standard incident value stream with some adaptations for specific circumstances such as VIP users or major incidents. Existing value streams need to be assessed when there is a new or changed service to ensure they are appropriate. Touchpoints with other practices need to be mapped. To create a value stream for user support, you will need to consider areas such as:

- Stakeholders;
- Internal or external resources;
- Escalation paths and work methods: dedicated, standby, swarming, self-support, shift-left*; and
- Hours and levels of support.

* **Shift-left** in a support context means moving knowledge closer to the customer to improve resolution times and customer experience (CX). This could be via frequently asked questions (FAQs) and self-service portals, via better trained front-line teams, or using approaches like swarming.

The figure below illustrates how ITIL's SVS is used in each step of the user support value stream.

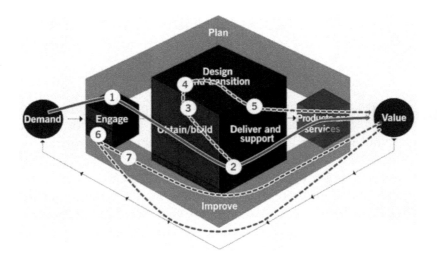

Figure 5: Restoration of a live service[10]

1. Acknowledge and record the user contact (engage).
2. Investigate the event, classify it as an incident, attempt to fix it (deliver and support).
3. Get a fix from the specialist team (obtain/build).
4. Apply the fix (design and transition).
5. Verify the fix resolved the situation (delivery and support).
6. Ask for user feedback (engage).
7. Identify improvement opportunities (improve).

Note there is a split in the activity line at step 2. If the issue is resolved, then value is restored. If not, then the activities follow the dashed line. The value stream could also end at

[10] *ITIL® 4: Create, Deliver and Support*, figure 4.12. Copyright © AXELOS Limited 2020. Used under permission of AXELOS Limited. All rights reserved.

step 5. It is common to collect feedback after the situation has been resolved.

There are several practices that might help to improve a user support value stream. Not all practices are examinable (examinable practices are in **bold**). The practices to improve a user support value stream include:

- **Incident management**
- **Service desk**
- Risk management
- **Knowledge management**
- Supplier management
- Service configuration management
- **Monitoring and event management**
- **Problem management**
- Software development and management
- Infrastructure and platform management
- Financial management
- Service validation and testing
- Deployment management
- Continual improvement
- **Service level management**

Using the Banksbest case study, map a value stream for an incident on the Mortbank system. Use the information in the case study and your own knowledge and experience to identify where there could be delays or improvement opportunities. What could be done differently?

CHAPTER 12: ITIL PRACTICES AND VALUE STREAMS FOR USER SUPPORT

This chapter addresses the development of a value stream for user support. The focus is on the ITIL practices that support the user support value stream. The practices are:

- Service desk
- Incident management
- Problem management
- Knowledge management
- Service level management
- Monitoring and event management

We'll review the practices in detail in the following chapters.

Scenario for user support

As most organisations have a fairly robust incident management process, let's check our understanding. Using the activities of the service value chain, the following activities occur:

- **Plan:** not engaged in this activity.
- **Engage:** acknowledge and register the user event; request feedback after a fix has been deployed.
- **Design and transition:** deploy the fix from the specialist team.
- **Obtain/build:** from specialist teams, create a fix – either permanent or a workaround.

- **Deliver and support:** confirm the event is an incident; attempt first-call resolution using past history; verify the incident has been resolved.
- **Improve**: identify opportunities to improve practice, process, service or component.

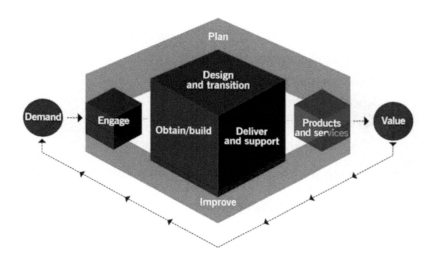

Figure 6: The service value chain[11]

Using the Banksbest case study, we will consider how the six practices would work together and provide user support. Here is the scenario:

Tom, a Banksbest mortgage customer, has called the customer service centre several times over the past week

---

[11] *ITIL® 4: Create, Deliver and Support*, figure 0.2. Copyright © AXELOS Limited 2020. Used under permission of AXELOS Limited. All rights reserved.

complaining that he has not been able to log in to his account, and when he has been able to log in, there is information missing. He is getting more and more frustrated as he is trying to complete his tax return.

Let's see how this situation is resolved using ITIL's practices.

- Tom contacts the Banksbest customer service centre to report his issue again.
- Carol, a customer service agent at Banksbest, listens carefully to Tom as he describes his issue.
- Carol opens a new ticket, prioritises it as urgent, and quickly looks at the history and activities that have been occurring. She sees that the Mortbank technical specialist for user accounts has been working on the issue. The technical specialist has found that Tom is not the only one who has experienced this issue. The technical specialist has found that Tom is not the only one who has experienced this issue, which is caused by users having multiple accounts.. The technical specialist has been working to consolidate these accounts for all affected users but hasn't gotten to Tom yet. Carol also sees a problem management ticket has been opened and is being worked on.

The problem management team is now investigating how multiple accounts could be created and are working on a solution. It is investigating how this could happen and working on a solution to ensure it can't happen in the future. This team has been using the data and information resources from knowledge management to review service designs and technical specifications for the Mortbank service.

In this encounter, the service desk practice engaged in the issue with empathy and provided good communication. Additionally, Carol provided a solution to Tom by verbally delivering the information he needed urgently, and Tom left the call with an excellent CX. Carol had been empowered by the organisation to go beyond typical activities to ensure a positive CX.

The incident management practice was being followed but, in this case, escalation and delivering a solution within the defined time frame (the service level management practice, specifically the Mortbank service level agreement (SLA)), didn't occur. Once this issue has been technically resolved, the incident management practice will look to improve its handling of multiple issues.

Problem management engaged once the service desk alerted them to the multiple occurrences of the same issue. The team then followed reactive problem management activities. In their investigation, data and information from the monitoring and event management practice (log files for Mortbank) and knowledge management practice (service design documentation) assisted in their understanding and solution development.

Based on the outcomes from the problem management investigation as well as the number of issues that were continuing to accumulate, the service level management practice initiated a review of the Mortbank SLA and began the process to update this service.

While Tom is only aware of his interaction with Carol, many practices worked on the issue simultaneously. An integrated

service management toolset allows the sharing of information and supports the collaborative nature of the work.

CHAPTER 13: VALUE STREAMS FOR USER SUPPORT: SERVICE DESK

This chapter explores key elements of the service desk practice. Those elements include:

- Purpose and description;
- Service empathy; and
- Practice success factors.

Purpose and description

Most of us have interacted with a service desk and we come away from that engagement with a positive or negative impression of the organisation. The service desk is often the first and only encounter we have with a service provider organisation – the other teams within the organisation are invisible to us. The service desk needs to deliver a great user experience (UX) and work to achieve high levels of customer satisfaction.

The purpose of the service desk is *"to capture demand for incident resolution and service requests. It should also be the entry point and single point of contact for the service provider for all users."*

An incident is *"an unplanned interruption to a service or reduction in the quality of a service."*

The service desk team typically supports multiple service management practices, including:

- Incident management
- Service request management

- Problem management
- Service configuration management
- Relationship management

These relationships are based on the direct contact and communication the service desk has with users. Any value stream activity that requires user communication will use the service desk.

Many service management practitioners, myself included, start their career working on a service desk. It's a common entry-level role in an IT organisation. Working on the service desk gives you a rapid introduction to the organisation and its services and allows you to quickly pick up technical knowledge to enable you to resolve common incidents. There are other benefits to working on a service desk. As the point of contact for the customer, you learn to judge the 'tone' of a conversation, prioritise and deal with conflict and anger on occasions. As we always used to say, no one rings the service desk to say "Thank you, everything is working fine!"

I still use skills that I learned on the service desk more than 20 years later. I would recommend that any service management practitioner spends time with their service desk colleagues, learning what the common issues are and getting a feel for overall customer satisfaction. It also provides an opportunity to improve the service desk analyst's day. A colleague of mine, for example, found that a one-off report he'd asked for was being produced every day, a highly manual task. He wasn't aware of this until he visited the service desk and was able to tell them to stop.

Service empathy

A critical characteristic of a service desk role is the ability to empathise. Service empathy is *"the ability to recognize, understand, predict, and project the interests, needs, intentions, and experiences of another party in order to establish, maintain, and improve the service relationship."* Service empathy is a critical element of user satisfaction and the success of the service provider.

Practice success factors

The service desk practice includes two PSFs:

- *"Enabling and continually improving effective, efficient, and convenient communications between the service provider and its users."*
- *"Enabling the effective integration of user communications into value streams."*

Enable and improve communication

Support channels for users should be easy to locate, easy to use, and provide the necessary support efficiently. The design of the user interface is determined by numerous factors, including:

- Service relationship model and type – is the relationship public or private, internal or external? Is the type of relationship basic, cooperative or a partnership?
- User profile – what are their capabilities based on location, age, culture, diversity, etc.?
- Service provider profile – what are their technical capabilities, user satisfaction strategy, etc.?
- External factors – consider the PESTLE impacts (political, economic, social, technological, legal, environmental).

The relationship types are:

- Basic: *"A basic relationship is usually appropriate for standard products and services, when the efficiency of service operation is a cornerstone."*
- Cooperative: *"In a cooperative service relationship, the service provider usually tailors the products and services to the service consumer needs. The customer expects that the service provider will think about service outcome and experience, not only service levels."*
- Partnership: *"In a partnership, the service provider and the service consumer may act as one organization coordinating activities across a great range of functions and processes. As the level of interdependency and integration grows, both parties may align on a strategic level by setting goals and priorities together."*

What type of relationship does Banksbest have with its business banking customers? What about its mortgage customers? How does the type of relationship influence the relationship management activities that Banksbest needs to carry out?

Due to advances in technology, communication channels for user support can be provided by a human or via technical solutions. Some examples of communication channels are shown in the table below:

Table 10: Communication Channels

Human	Technology
Voice	Web portals
Live chat	Interactive voice menus
Email	Mobile applications
Walk-in	Chatbots

Typically, service providers will use multiple channels to provide user support. These channels should be connected and integrated, or 'omnichannel'. Omnichannel describes *"unified communications across multiple channels based on sharing information across the channels and providing a seamless communication experience."*

Omnichannel communication allows the user to start a support call using a mobile application to create an appointment, follow up with a call to the service desk, and then have a solution applied by a technician without needing to provide the same information at each progressive stage.

Multichannel communication that is not integrated could require information to be entered at each stage with a risk of creating gaps in the support actions, or losing or corrupting information.

Integrating user communication into value streams

The service desk provides bi-directional communication between the service provider and the user. The service desk practice focuses on accurately capturing, recording and integrating communication into relevant value streams.

One example of communication by the service provider to the user would be a notification around planned changes. The content, format and timing of the message is determined by change enablement and release management practices, but the service desk establishes and maintains the communication channel.

Think about the service provider organisations that you interact with in your personal life – perhaps online banking, insurance providers, or smart devices in your home. What communication do you receive from the service providers? Is the communication effective? Do you know how to contact them when you need to?

User-initiated communication (such as queries) must be triaged by the service desk, to allow it to be forwarded to the appropriate value stream. Once forwarded, the relevant value stream processes and acts upon the query following specific processes and procedures.

The concept of triage comes from a military medical context. It focuses on identifying the most urgent work so it can be dealt with first. Low-priority work has to wait until high- and medium-priority work has been completed. Triage can be used to manage workloads such as development backlogs and incident queues. However, it's important to make sure the low-priority work doesn't get forgotten about..

CHAPTER 14: VALUE STREAMS FOR USER SUPPORT: INCIDENT MANAGEMENT

In this chapter, we explore key elements of the incident management practice. Those elements include:

- Purpose and description;
- Terms and concepts;
- Practice success factors; and
- Incident handling and resolution.

Purpose and description

Incident management is probably the most well-known service management process – everyone has experienced some sort of technical failure that has needed resolution. That is exactly what the incident management practice does. The purpose of incident management is: *"to minimize the negative impact of incidents by restoring normal service operation as quickly as possible."* An incident is defined as *"an unplanned interruption to a service or reduction in the quality of a service."*

Notice the purpose is very clear – restore service as quickly as possible; minimise the impact of an incident. These are important statements – incident management is about service **restoration** and not necessarily finding the cause or developing a permanent fix. Those activities fall within the scope of the problem management practice.

Another key word in the purpose is 'normal'. What does normal mean? Normal operation is defined in the technical specification for the service or within the configuration item

(CI – *"Any component that needs to be managed in order to deliver an IT service."*). The takeaway here is that the service should operate as expected and as agreed. When it doesn't, the incident management practice works to achieve a quick restoration of service. This helps to:

- Achieve user and customer satisfaction;
- Maintain or improve the credibility of the service provider; and
- Maintain or improve value co-creation.

Terms and concepts

Two factors enable the achievement of the incident management purpose:

- Early incident detection.
- Quick restoration of normal operations.

Both factors are made possible with well-defined processes and procedures, automation (think about the monitoring and event management practice), good supplier relationships (not all service components are solely owned by the service provider) and properly trained and skilled specialist teams.

Incidents are rarely unique – there are definite patterns and trends within some services. These incidents that are understood and can be resolved are related to known errors and will have a workaround (temporary solution) associated with them.

Organisations will develop incident models to optimise the handling and resolution of repeating incidents. Models support efficiency (quick restoration of service) by applying a proven and tested solution (the workaround).

Some of the key definitions you need to understand are:

- **Known error:** *"A problem that has been analyzed but has not been resolved."* (This is related to the problem management practice.)
- **Workaround:** *"A solution that reduces or eliminates the impact of an incident or problem for which a full resolution is not yet available. Some workarounds reduce the likelihood of incidents."* (This is related to the problem management practice.)
- **Incident model:** *"A repeatable approach to the management of a particular type of incident."*

Some incidents will dramatically effect service operation, causing severe performance issues, unavailability and potentially negatively impact user and customer satisfaction. These are known as major incidents – *"an incident with significant business impact requiring an immediate coordinated resolution."*

Major incidents have significant business impact – the key deliverable of an organisation is not available. For example, at the Minute Maid plant, the question at the service desk when a call comes in is, "Is juice still flowing?" If it is, it is not considered a major incident.

A major incident model can be created to clearly define what is a major incident and what isn't. Other characteristics of this model include:

- A named coordinator and a dedicated team (in place only when the major incident is active);
- Other dedicated resources (such as budget!);

- A communication model; and
- An agreed procedure for review and follow-up activities.

Imagine you work in the service management department at Banksbest. The customer service centre has reported that Bizbank isn't working. They are struggling to log in, and when they do manage to log in, key functions are timing out.

What steps would you follow? Who would you work with? Try to map the major incident through to resolution, using the case study and your own experience.

The use of workarounds is common practice within incident management. A workaround allows for the quick restoration of service at an acceptable level of quality. However, continued application of workarounds can increase technical debt (defined as *"the total rework backlog accumulated by choosing workarounds instead of system solutions that would take longer."*) and may lead to future incidents. The problem management practice is responsible for identifying the root cause of an incident or group of incidents and then developing a solution to overcome them. These actions will reduce the technical debt caused by incident management workarounds.

Practice success factors

There are three PSFs for incident management:

- Detect incidents early.
- Resolve incidents quickly and efficiently.
- Continually improve the practice.

Detect incidents early

Historically, the most common method of detecting incidents was by collecting information from users or technical specialists. Now, automation can detect and register incidents (for more information, see the monitoring and event management practice). Why is automation useful? The benefits include:

- Earlier detection (leading to decreased service downtime);
- Higher quality initial data leads to faster resolution time (including the trigger for self-healing);
- Some incidents may not be seen by users – they will be 'seen' by automated methods before they impact user experience;
- Some incidents are resolved before they impact agreed service quality; and
- Incident cost decreases due to earlier resolution and reduced impact.

Automation may be improved with the advances in machine learning. Learning from past incidents, events, known errors and other sources can improve incident detection and categorisation. Self-healing systems offer automated resolution.

The incident management practice includes categorisation. This is the act of assigning a category to something. For example, an incident will be categorised as low, medium or high priority depending on its impact and urgency.

The key to success for the incident management practice is early detection. What if there are no automated technologies available? In this situation, aim to develop and promote a culture of responsible service consumption and encourage the reporting of suspicious events. Remember value is co-created – users should be encouraged to report unusual occurrences as quickly as possible.

Resolve incidents quickly and efficiently

If incidents are detected early and then the resolution is delayed, where's the value? Consider the following situations and the benefits they will bring:

- Recurring and simple incidents have pre-defined resolutions that may be automated or standardised via a proven model.
- Complex situations where the system is well known are escalated to the specialist group for diagnosis and resolution.
- Very complex situations where it's impossible to define which specialist group should handle the incident deploy a collective approach called 'swarming'.

Escalation is defined as *"an activity that obtains additional resources in order to meet service targets or customer expectations."* Swarming is *"a technique for solving various complex tasks. In swarming, multiple people with different areas of expertise work together on a task until it becomes clear which competencies are the most relevant and needed."*

The purpose of swarming is to decrease the level of complexity of the (possibly major) incident by having numerous specialists involved in the individual investigation and resolution activities. This way, specialists with the correct expertise can work on elements of the incident rather than a generic group trying to solve the incident as a whole. Physical meetings are typically avoided with swarming, allowing the specialists to experiment and design scripts and other tools for discovery activities. No matter what technique is used to resolve incidents quickly, ensure the data being analysed is correct and accurate.

While incidents should be resolved as soon as possible, the resources to perform all of the necessary work may not be available. Prioritisation is essential. Note the difference between the following definitions:

- **Task priority** – *"the importance of a task relative to other tasks. Tasks with higher priority are worked on first. Priority is defined based on all the tasks in the backlog."*
- **Prioritisation** – *"selecting tasks to work on first when it's impossible to assign resources to all tasks in the backlog."*

Some rules for prioritisation include:

- Defining the impact and urgency of an incident is not prioritisation, but their estimation supports prioritisation.

- Prioritisation is only needed when there is a resource conflict.
- Incidents should be processed with other tasks in a single backlog.
- Prioritisation is used to assign people to tasks; those teams will estimate processing time and resource availability. Even with target resolution times defined in an SLA, teams can override those targets if, in their estimation, the current incident has a greater impact than what was expected when the SLA was agreed.

In my experience, prioritisation can be an extremely challenging exercise. A software patch, for example, might deliver no change from the end user perspective, but the security team believes it is essential. Does this mean the work is more or less important than a failing service? Technical teams might be accused of 'cherry picking' the incidents that look interesting to work on, leaving more mundane tasks for later.

The important consideration for prioritisation is to have clear, transparent guidance. Save time and energy by setting clear standards – this also improves relationships as arguments reduce!

Visualisation tools (such as Kanban and Lean principles) can be used to help limit work in progress and support prioritisation.

To help identify impact, consider the direct effect of an incident (or problem) on the business (e.g. who was impacted? Where? When?). Urgency can be assessed by considering how much time is available to resolve the incident (or problem) before the business is negatively affected.

Continually improve the practice

Reviewing incident management records at regular intervals helps to identify areas for improvement as well as areas that are working well. Additionally, knowledge sharing between specialist teams creates efficiencies that may improve existing or introduce new incident models. Reviews also allow analysis of stakeholder satisfaction with the incident management practice. Good-quality data is essential to the review process. Data should be concurrent, complete and comprehensive:

- **Concurrent:** Data that describes exactly what was done and when, to assist in continual improvement. This requires stakeholders to update incident records during the event, not after. An accurate timeline is useful for investigation.
- **Complete:** Ensure data accurately describes what activities have been done.
- **Comprehensive:** Describe why activities were done (this can be as important as the initial description).

Incident handling and resolution

Review the figure 7[12] and table 11.

[12] *ITIL® 4: Practice Guide: Incident Management*, figure 3.2. Copyright © AXELOS Limited 2020. Used under permission of AXELOS Limited. All rights reserved.

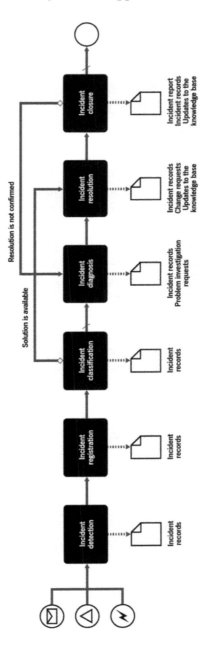

Figure 7: Workflow of the incident handling and resolution process

Table 11: Incident Management[13]

Activity	Manually processed user-detected incidents	Automatically detected and processed incidents
Incident detection	The user detects a malfunction in service operation and contacts the service provider's service desk via the agreed channel(s). The service desk agent performs the initial triage of the user query, confirming that the query does indeed refer to an incident.	An event is detected by a monitoring system and identified as an incident based on a pre-defined classification.
Incident registration	The service desk agent performs incident registration, adding the available data to the incident record.	An incident record is registered and associated with the CI where the event has been detected. Pre-defined technical data is registered. If

[13] *ITIL® 4 Practice Guide: Incident Management*, table 3.2. Copyright © AXELOS Limited 2020. Used under permission of AXELOS Limited. All rights reserved.

		needed, a notification is sent to the relevant technical specialists.
Incident classification	*The service desk agent performs initial classification of the incident; this helps to qualify incident impact, identify the team responsible for the failed CIs and/or services, and to link the incident to other past and ongoing events, incidents, and/or problems.* *In some cases, classification helps to reveal a previously defined solution for this type of incident.*	*Based on pre-defined rules, the following is automatically discovered:* • *the incident's impact on services and users* • *the solutions available* • *the technical team(s) responsible for the incident resolution, if automated solutions are ineffective or unavailable.*
Incident diagnosis	*If classification does not provide an understanding of a solution, technical*	*If the automated solution is ineffective or unavailable, the incident is*

	specialist teams perform incident diagnosis. This may involve escalation of the incident between the teams, or joint techniques, such as swarming. If classification is wrong because of an incorrect CI assignment, this information should be communicated to those responsible for configuration control (see the service configuration practice guide).	*escalated to the responsible technical team for manual diagnosis. It may involve escalation of the incident between the teams, or joint techniques, such as swarming. If an automated solution failed because of an incorrect CI association, this information should be communicated to those responsible for the configuration control (see the service configuration practice guide).*
Incident resolution	*When a solution is found, the relevant specialist teams attempt to apply it, working sequentially or in parallel. It may require the*	*If there is an automated solution available, it is applied, tested, and confirmed. If a manual intervention is required, a*

	initiation of a change. If the solution does not work, additional diagnosis is performed.	*relevant specialist team attempts to apply it. It may require the initiation of a change. If the solution proves not to work, additional diagnosis is performed.*
Incident closure	*After the incident is successfully resolved, a number of formal closure procedures may be needed:* • *user confirmation of service restoration* • *resolution costs calculation and reporting* • *resolution price calculation and invoicing* • *problem investigation initiation* • *incident review.*	*If the automated solution proves effective, incident records are automatically updated and closed. A report is sent to the responsible technical team. If information about the incident has been communicated to other stakeholders at any of the previous steps, the closure of the incident should also be communicated.*

	After all the required actions are completed and the incident records are updated accordingly, the incident is formally closed. This can be done by the product owner, service owner, incident manager, or service desk agent, depending on the agreed incident model.	

CHAPTER 15: VALUE STREAMS FOR USER SUPPORT: PROBLEM MANAGEMENT

In this chapter, we explore key elements of the problem management practice. Those elements include:

- Purpose and description;
- Problem identification;
- Practice success factors;
- Proactive problem identification; and
- Reactive problem identification.

Purpose and description

In the previous chapter, we studied the incident management practice. The problem management practice works closely with incident management.

The purpose of problem management is *"to reduce the likelihood and impact of incidents by identifying actual and potential causes of incidents and managing workarounds and known errors."*

With any service, perfection is rare, and incidents will occur. While the incident management practice will manage incidents and try to restore service, the problem management practice will try to identify and manage the **cause** of the incident. A problem is *"a cause, or potential cause, of one or more incidents."*

Terms and concepts

There are three phases to the problem management practice:

- Problem identification.
- Problem control (non-examinable – read more in the problem management practice guide after your exam if this area is relevant to your role).
- Error control (non-examinable).

There is an evolution that takes place from a problem to an error.

Problem identification has two elements:

- **Reactive problem management** – investigates the causes of incidents that have already occurred, to try and prevent incidents recurring.
- **Proactive problem management** – identifies problems before an incident is caused, assesses the related risks and creates a response that minimises the possibility of an incident or reduces its potential impact. Information sources for proactive problem management include vendor communication (vulnerabilities in their products); developers, designers or testers discovering errors in live versions; user communities; monitoring data; and technical audits.

Practice success factors

There are two PSFs for the problem management practice:

- *"Identify and understand problems and their impact on services"*

  When organisations understand the errors in their products and services, incidents can be mitigated or even prevented. Problem management ensures problem identification, contributing to continual improvement of products and services.

- *"Optimize problem resolution and mitigation."*

  Once problems are identified, manage them appropriately. Not all problems can be removed (or need to be removed) – problems should be permanently resolved, balancing costs, risks and impact on service quality.

Proactive problem management

Proactive problem management identifies problems before an incident occurs. The table below defines the key inputs, activities and key outputs.

Table 12: Problem Management[14]

Key Inputs	*Activities*	*Key Outputs*
• *Error information from vendors and suppliers* • *Information about potential errors submitted by specialist teams*	• *Review of the submitted information* • *Problem registration* • *Initial problem categorization and assignment*	• *Problem records* • *Feedback to the problem initiator*

---

[14] *ITIL® 4 Practice Guide: Problem Management,* table 3.1. Copyright © AXELOS Limited 2020. Used under permission of AXELOS Limited. All rights reserved.

• *Information about potential errors submitted by external user and professional communities* • *Information about potential errors submitted by users* • *Monitoring data* • *Service configuration data*		

The workflow for the proactive problem identification process is shown below.

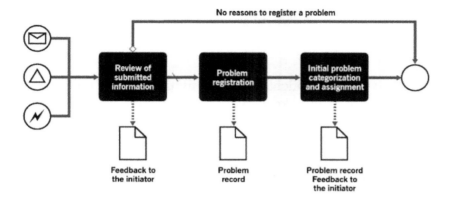

Figure 8: Workflow of the proactive problem identification process[15]

The review of the submitted information is completed by a specialist. They will ensure:

- The submitted information doesn't duplicate a current problem record; and
- It's applicable to the organisation.

If it is related to ongoing incidents, the problem would be registered at this point or rejected (with a notification to the submitter). To register the problem, a problem record is created. During the record creation, the problem is given an initial categorisation. The initial categorisation is based on the information submitted and the output of the initial review. The problem is then assigned to a specialist group that is responsible for the presumed configuration item, service or product at fault. Problem categorisation can

---

[15] *ITIL® 4 Practice Guide: Problem Management*, figure 3.2. Copyright © AXELOS Limited 2020. Used under permission of AXELOS Limited. All rights reserved.

change as the technical specialist investigates and uncovers more information.

Proactive problem identification activities identify potential errors in products and services. Information used in this discovery includes sources other than incident records. Additional information sources include vendor communication (vulnerabilities in their products); developers, designers or testers discovering errors in live versions; user communities; monitoring data; and technical audits.

Proactive problem identification is a form of risk management. The activities include identification, assessment and analysis of vulnerabilities and associated risks. The focus of proactive problem management should be key systems and components that could cause the highest impact to the organisation if they failed. In the assessment of the possible problems, consider the probability and impact of the identified vulnerabilities. Proactive problem management activities link to continual improvement activities and will provide inputs to the work carried out there.

Reactive problem identification

The workflow for the reactive problem identification process is below.

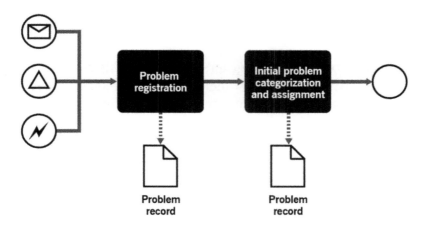

Figure 9: Workflow of the reactive problem identification process[16]

Problem registration during reactive problem identification is triggered by an ongoing incident. It could be a single incident that has significant impact, or multiple incidents across the enterprise. A problem could also be registered after the resolution of the incident. Initial problem categorisation and assignment of the problem record would be completed by the person registering the problem. The information that should be included is:

- Description;
- Associated configuration items;
- Estimated impact and probability of incidents;
- Associated/potentially affected services; and
- Impact to the organisation and customers.

---

[16] *ITIL® 4 Practice Guide: Problem Management*, figure 3.3. Copyright © AXELOS Limited 2020. Used under permission of AXELOS Limited. All rights reserved.

The problem is then assigned to the appropriate specialist group.

Problems could also be registered by an analysis of incident records. Based on those incidents, the specialist team reviewing them may decide to register a problem record. The justification could be a high number of similar incidents, major incidents, poor availability, among others. When registering a problem based on incident analysis, the analyst performs categorisation and includes similar information to the ongoing incident activity. The record is assigned to an appropriate specialist group based on associated CI, service or product.

Reactive problem identification uses information from past and ongoing incidents, as well as monitoring data, configuration data and SLAs. The key inputs, activities and key outputs of reactive problem identification are shown in the table below.

Table 13: Problem Management[17]

Key Inputs	*Activities*	*Key Outputs*
• *Information about ongoing incidents* • *Incident records and reports* • *Monitoring data*	• *Problem registration* • *Initial problem categorization and assignment*	• *Problem records*

[17] *ITIL® 4 Practice Guide: Problem Management,* table 3.2. Copyright © AXELOS Limited 2020. Used under permission of AXELOS Limited. All rights reserved.

Service configuration data *Service level agreements (SLAs)*		

The incident management and problem management practices are used within a single value stream and will share the same resources (including teams, tools and procedures). Methods used in problem identification include statistical analysis, impact analysis and trend analysis. These techniques allow for the identification of common causes.

I've worked with several organisations that have started formal problem management activities and found themselves quickly overwhelmed. Letting other teams know that there is an area responsible for investigating long-term issues can create a dumping ground for all the difficult things that have been hanging around – sometimes for years!

It can be helpful to use a pain value to prioritise what needs to be done. For each problem or potential problem, think about:

- The volume of incidents;
- The number of customers who are affected;

- The length of time it takes to resolve incidents (and therefore the associated cost);
- The cost to the business of the time that is lost; and
- The impact to the customer or user experience.

This exercise can be done relatively quickly by a group working together and can help to identify quick wins and serious issues.

CHAPTER 16: VALUE STREAMS FOR USER SUPPORT: KNOWLEDGE MANAGEMENT

In this chapter, we explore key elements of the knowledge management practice. Those elements include:

- Purpose and description;
- The SECI model of knowledge dimensions; and
- Practice success factors.

Purpose and description

The knowledge management practice provides a method, structure, and culture for the development, collection, processing and analysis of data, information and knowledge across all value streams and practices. Every value stream and practice benefits from the knowledge management practice. Its purpose is *"to maintain and improve the effective, efficient, and convenient use of information and knowledge across the organization."*

Simply put, knowledge management aims to provide the right information, to the right person, at the right time.

The activities within the knowledge management practice transform information and organisational intellectual capital into value for employees and service customers. To accomplish this, there must be an established and integrated process for managing knowledge assets. Additionally, people must be empowered to develop and share knowledge.

Two premises exist for the knowledge management practice:

- Knowledge is processed and used in every value stream and as such, information must be available and on time.

- The focus of this practice is on the discovery and provision of high-quality information, meaning information is available, accurate, reliable, relevant, complete, timely and compliant.

SECI model of knowledge dimensions

The ability to learn is critical to people and organisations, especially when innovation and the ability to change dominate today's environment. The organisation's absorptive capacity must be continuously developed through the creation and use of new knowledge. Absorptive capacity is *"the organization's ability to recognize the value of new information, to embed it into an existing knowledge system, and to apply it to the achievement of business outcomes."*

The SECI (socialisation, externalisation, combination, internalisation) model of knowledge dimensions describes knowledge sharing and the transformation process across any organisation.

Two types of knowledge form the basis of this model:

- **Explicit knowledge:** *"Knowledge transferred to others, codified, assessed, verbalized, and stored. It includes information from books, databases, descriptions, and so on."*

- **Tacit knowledge:** *"Knowledge that is difficult to transfer to others, difficult to express, codify, and assess. It is based on experience, values, capabilities, and skills."*

According to the SECI model, there are two dimensions for knowledge creation:

- Converting tacit knowledge to explicit knowledge and vice versa.
- Transferring knowledge from an individual to a group(s) or organisation.

Knowledge is used through socialisation, externalisation, internalisation, or through a combination approach:

- **Socialisation:** Tacit-to-tacit sharing; knowledge is shared face-to-face or through experiences (coaching, mentoring).
- **Externalisation:** Tacit-to-explicit sharing; experiences are described or formulated in documentation.
- **Internalisation:** Explicit-to-tacit sharing; an individual develops their knowledge independently or through formal training.
- **Combination:** Explicit-to-explicit sharing; data from internal and external sources is combined, analysed, and presented to form new knowledge.

Using and exchanging knowledge happens continually. The knowledge management practice must recognise the continuity and evolution of knowledge. Remember, the purpose of knowledge is to support data-driven decisions ("I know" vs "I think" decisions).

Practice success factors

The knowledge management practice has two PSFs:

- *"Creation and maintenance of knowledge and its transfer and use across an organization*

- *Effective use of information for decision-making across an organization"*

Creation and maintenance of knowledge and its transfer and use across an organization

There must be an effective culture around knowledge sharing that is developed, maintained and supported. The knowledge management practice describes tools and techniques that will only be effective in a nurturing culture – one where the organisation embraces the need to identify, understand, use, analyse, learn, unlearn, transfer, present and discuss data and information in a way that supports the organisational mission, vision and strategy.

Knowledge can be a competitive advantage and as such, knowledge transfer can run into many barriers. Stakeholders must stress the value and importance of sharing knowledge and create the appropriate atmosphere to support knowledge transfer.

Here's a common scenario. You have a question, and you spend quite a long time finding the answer. You need to check information stores inside the organisation and eventually you give up and search the Internet. As you describe your frustration to a colleague, they say "Why didn't you ask me? I could have told you that!"

The result? Even more frustration! Every day, people in organisations all over the world waste hundreds of thousands of hours looking for information that exists but is difficult to find. Knowledge management is an essential organisational capability and underpins the adoption of technologies like AI and ML.

Effective use of information for decision-making

A successful knowledge management practice develops not only the tools and techniques to collect and maintain knowledge but also people. The development of a knowledge culture is crucial to the practice.

Successful organisations work to develop the competencies to use, collect and share information throughout the organisation. Information quality is paramount to their operation – not only for good decision-making, but also as a performance measure of the practice.

When designing a knowledge management system, consider the following errors and design to overcome them:

- Errors in the information collection (poor data entry).
- No alignment or integration between internal and external sources (no consistency in format or entry standards).
- Lost information due to unstructured data storage.
- Loss of data during migrations.
- Difficult-to-use interfaces (poor tool to support data search).

Remember, the purpose of data is to support effective decision-making. Data describes the past. Decisions are typically predicting the future. As data is being collated and analysed, intuition and the creative thinking skills of an individual are combined with the power of forecasting tools. This mixture creates possible alternatives and then the best solution. The quality of the decision is directly related to the quality of the data.

CHAPTER 17: VALUE STREAMS FOR USER SUPPORT: SERVICE LEVEL MANAGEMENT

In this chapter, we explore key elements of the service level management practice. Those elements include:

- Purpose and description;
- Scope; and
- Practice success factors.

Purpose and description

The service level management practice creates and manages a shared view of quality services between the service provider and consumer. The purpose of service level management is *"to set clear business-based targets for service levels, and to ensure that delivery of services is properly assessed, monitored, and managed against these targets."*

The shared view is documented (normally in a service level agreement (SLA)) and the focus is on service quality and value. Service agreements are in place throughout the entire service relationship. An SLA is *"a documented agreement between a service provider and a customer that identifies both services required and the expected level of service."*

The key activities of the service level management practice are shown in figure 10.

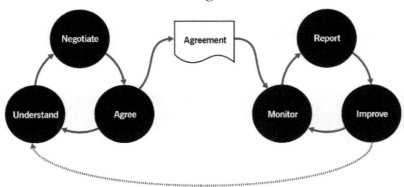

Figure 10: Key activities of the service level management practice[18]

The service level management practice scope includes:

- Tactical and operational communication with customers about expected, agreed and actual service quality;
- Negotiating, agreeing and maintaining SLAs with customers;
- Understanding the design and architecture of services and their dependencies;
- Continual review of achieved service levels versus agreed and expected; and
- Initiation of service improvements (applied to agreements, monitoring, reporting, service performance)

---

[18] *ITIL® 4 Practice Guide: Service Level Management,* figure 2.1. Copyright © AXELOS Limited 2020. Used under permission of AXELOS Limited. All rights reserved.

Service levels are defined as *"one or more metrics that define expected or achieved service quality."*

There are several activities in other service management practices that support the service level management practice. The practices and their associated activities are shown in the table below.

Table 14: Service Level Management[19]

Activity	*Practice Guide*
Strategic communications with customers and sponsors	*Relationship management*
Operational communications with users	*Service desk*
Establishing and managing of contracts with suppliers and partners	*Supplier management*
Identification and documentation of services	*Service catalogue management*
Design of products and services	*Service design*
Analysis of innovation opportunities and new	*Business analysis*

---

[19] *ITIL® 4 Practice Guide: Service Level Management*, table 2.1. Copyright © AXELOS Limited 2020. Used under permission of AXELOS Limited. All rights reserved.

requirements for services outside of existing utility and warranty options	
Design and control of financial models for commercial service delivery	*Service financial management*
Ongoing management and implementation of improvements	*Continual improvement*
Implementation of changes to products and services	*Change enablement* *Project management* *Other practices*
Monitoring technology, team and supplier performance	*Monitoring and event management*

I've worked with some organisations whose SLA efforts failed because the agreements were created with the wrong intention. Agreement is the key word; SLAs don't exist to force targets onto one party or the other.

I worked with one organisation that was unhappy with how a particular service was performing. The SLA was driven by the customer, who wanted to create targets that couldn't be met without significant investment (and no funds were made available). The team that owned the service became more focused on creating reports that would meet the targets than they were on actually improving the service.

SLAs must be a joint effort, and the relationship between the parties who sign the SLA requires continual maintenance and nurturing.

Practice success factors

There are four PSFs for service level management:

- *"Establishing a shared view of target service levels with customers"*
- *"Overseeing how the organization meets the defined service levels through the collection, analysis, storage, and reporting of the relevant metrics for the identified services"*
- *"Performing service reviews to ensure that the current set of services continues to meet the needs of the organization and its customers"*
- *"Capturing and reporting on improvement opportunities, including performance against defined service levels and stakeholder satisfaction."*

Establishing a shared view of target service levels

Customer interactions will differ depending on the service relationship model – consider a tailored or 'out of the box' relationship. The 'out of the box' customer will need to accept the available service levels (or will have minimal opportunities for negotiation). A tailored service offers greater flexibility in defining the service level targets. Not all targets have to be agreed before the service is delivered and consumed; the SLA can and should evolve over time.

To establish a tailored service, the customer's needs and expectations are the main discussion point. It's important to ensure that the customer (including users and sponsors) and service provider (represented by service delivery teams, service provision sponsors, service architects, service designers, business analysist, and service development teams) agree to the service specifications. As discussions progress, the scope of service quality is refined and narrowed until it represents a service level that can be delivered at the necessary levels of assurance and liability.

In 'out of the box' services, service levels are typically predefined. These definitions come from analysing the market to create a generic profile for a specific service. There might be a tiered service delivery available (gold, silver and bronze, for example) for those who wish to use (and pay for) variations to the service levels.

Regardless of the relationship type, all service levels should have a clear method for measurement and reporting. If possible, define the metrics early and ensure measurement and reporting tools are integrated into the service. Metrics that measure overall service quality include functionality, availability, performance, timeliness, user support, accuracy and user experience (UX) measures.

What happens when the agreed service level quality differs from the expected quality levels? This is where good relationship management skills are needed. The ITIL guiding principles can also help develop a mutually shared view of service quality.

Overseeing how the organization meets the defined service levels

Once the service level targets are established, services are delivered and consumed. The service provider should control the quality of the service keeping in mind these three perspectives:

- Achieved service level – compared to what was agreed.
- User satisfaction – feedback from the service desk, surveys, etc.
- Customer satisfaction – feedback from reviews, surveys, social media comments, etc.

The practice will collect, store, analyse and report on this data to relevant stakeholders from both provider and consumer perspectives. One point to note is that service level management does not design or execute data collection. Other practices, specifically service design, monitoring and event management, and measurement and reporting, will perform this work. The service level management practice will make sense of the data and then communicate and review with stakeholders.

Performing service reviews

The purpose of a service review is to share the achieved service quality information and discuss the value enabled by the service. As a result, service improvements may be initiated.

Service reviews may be one of two types:

- **Event based:** This type of review is triggered by events (major incidents, a request for a significant change to a service, a change in business need, etc.).
- **Interval based:** This type of review is scheduled at regular and agreed time periods. The interval between meetings is usually based on previous satisfaction with the service, the number of changes to the service, and the likelihood of changes to the service expectations or requirements. The typical time frame is monthly but should be no longer than every three months.

No matter what the form of the review and when it takes place, service reviews are critical in the service relationship. There is a distinct relationship between the quality of a service review and the quality of the services and stakeholder satisfaction. Additionally, service reviews are an important source of service improvements, which is the next PSF.

Capturing and reporting on improvement opportunities

Service reviews provide the opportunity to improve services – based on underperformance of the service or to improve the level of satisfaction from users and customers. Of course, improvements can also be made to practices, processes, tools or other resources. Transparency is critical with improvements – ensure that any improvement suggestion is visible so that those who have made the suggestion know that it has been considered. This promotes the ITIL guiding principle of 'collaborate and promote visibility'.

All improvements to a product or service are owned by the accountable role (product owner or service owner). For effective implementation of practice, product and service improvements, follow the guidance in the continual improvement practice.

CHAPTER 18: VALUE STREAMS FOR USER SUPPORT: MONITORING AND EVENT MANAGEMENT

In this chapter, we explore key elements of the monitoring and event management practice. Those elements include:

- Purpose and description; and
- Practice success factors.

Purpose and description

The purpose of monitoring and event management is *"to systematically observe services and service components, and record and report selected changes of state identified as events."*

Activities for this practice include the identification and categorisation (analysis) of events throughout the infrastructure and between a service and its customers. This practice has two parts:

- **Monitoring** focuses on services and their components to detect changes of state that have significance. This information is communicated to relevant parties.
- **Event management** manages the identified events from monitoring activities and initiates the correct response to the event.

An event is defined as *"any change of state that has significance for the management of a service or other configuration item (CI)."* Monitoring describes *"repeated observation of a system, practice, process, service, or other entity to detect events and to ensure that the current status is known."*

Monitoring proactively observes designated services and service components and reports any changes of state (alert) as an event. These alerts are defined by predetermining thresholds for the monitored components that when breached, will trigger a response. The action taken will depend on the classification of the event. Typical categories, in order of increasing significance, are informational, warning and exception. These are explained below:

- Alert: *"A notification that a threshold has been reached, something has changed, or a failure has occurred."*
- Threshold: *"The value of a metric that triggers a pre-defined response."*
- Informational: *"Informational events provide the status of a device or service or confirm the state of a task and do not require action at the time they were identified."*
- Warning: *"A warning allows action to be taken before any negative impact is experienced. Warning events signify that an unusual, but not exceptional, operation is occurring."*
- Exception: *"Indicates that a critical threshold for a service or component metric has been reached, indicating failure, significant performance degradation, or loss of functionality."*

Monitoring and event management can be a highly specialised and technical area, but its consequences have a human impact. I worked with one organisation with oversensitive event management. Technical specialists who were on call were getting woken up at 2:00 am to be notified about something that didn't need immediate attention. Resolving the problem with the event types meant they got some sleep, and from a business perspective were able to perform much better during their normal working hours.

Practice success factors

There are three PSFs for monitoring and event management. They are to:

- *"Establish and maintain approaches/models that describe the various types of events and monitoring capabilities needed to detect them."*
- *"Ensure that timely, relevant, and sufficient monitoring data is available to relevant stakeholders."*
- *"Ensure that events are detected, interpreted, and if needed acted upon as quickly as possible."*

Establish and maintain approaches and models

Monitoring and event management has a significant challenge within its activities: data collection. The practice must plan its approach and the models it develops to collect data. There is always a risk of collecting too much data. The intent should be to collect just enough meaningful information to support service management activities across the organisation. To accomplish this PSF:

- Identify and prioritise services and the components that are monitored. This decision is based on the business objectives and the dependency of the components to achieve them.

- Balance the need for information, the granularity of the data and the frequency with which it is collected. The more data that is collected, the less information will be produced, if only due to the amount of data and the effort required to filter and analyse it. Automation and machine learning are useful tools to deploy for data analysis.

- Maintain an appropriate level of technology to collect, analyse, report and store monitored data. Define policies to address different types of events and their associated responses.

Ensure that data is available to stakeholders

Data that is relevant and timely allows fact-based decisions and actions. This is critical for the delivery of high-quality services (meeting service performance requirements) and continual improvement activities (identification of underperforming areas). Ensure this data is available to relevant stakeholders. For example, data from monitoring and event management can answer these questions from different stakeholder perspectives:

- **Service provider** – is the service performing as designed? Benchmark the service against the design specifications.
- **Customer** – am I getting what I paid for? Data showing performance has met (or not met) agreed service levels.
- **Customer and service provider** – who's at fault? Data can show where, for example, the customer is causing service faults and there is a need for training.

Ensure events are detected, interpreted and acted on as quickly as possible

The last PSF focuses on the efficiency of detecting events and then acting on them. The practices within monitoring and event management can be clearly defined, but if the architecture design and/or age of the components are overly complex or not compatible to modern monitoring tools, this practice will not provide the benefits it should. Monitoring and event management is heavily dependent on technology. Organisations should exploit the capabilities of technological advances – including automation, AI and ML to reduce the need for manual collection, analysis and reporting.

CHAPTER 19: HOW TO CREATE, DELIVER AND SUPPORT SERVICES

The final section of the ITIL 4 Specialist Create, Deliver and Support syllabus considers concepts around the creation, delivery and support of services. This information adds some detail to the previous chapters where we explored the use of a value stream to create a new service as well as to offer user support.

This chapter includes:

- Knowing how to coordinate, prioritise and structure work and activities to create, deliver and support services; and
- Understanding the use and value of three concepts and their impact to the SVS:
  - Buy vs build.
  - Sourcing options.
  - Service integration and management.

The concepts in this chapter are more generic in nature and evolve from organisational governance. For example, the decision to buy or build applications will typically be made based on a corporate policy on obtaining goods or services. Of course, the organisational capabilities to develop an application would also be considered. The same argument could be made for sourcing – what is the policy for sourcing and what parameters are included (e.g. sustainability, local first, culture, source must have an ISO/IEC 20000-1 certificate, etc.)?

The other areas that are covered in this chapter include managing work as tickets, prioritisation, and service integration and management. An important element of CDS is understanding how to coordinate, prioritise and structure work and activities as part of service delivery and support. This includes:

- Managing work as tickets; and
- Prioritising work.

Managing work as tickets

A 'ticket' system has traditionally been at the heart of any service management workflow. Each ticket represents a record of work and as each step of the workflow is completed, the ticket is passed to the next owner's inbox or filed if the workflow was complete. Frustrating the user is **not** the purpose of a ticketing system – tickets are important as they provide valuable information about the workflow. A ticket should never be the focus of the user experience.

For a service provider, a high volume of tickets and the associated queues don't have to lead to a poor customer experience. The service provider needs to focus on:

- Giving reliable information and status updates;
- Keeping users engaged;
- Requesting information from users to keep them involved; and
- Setting and meeting expectations.

Inefficient workflow management creates queues and bottlenecks or a backlog of tickets. Queues and bottlenecks interrupt the flow of work, and overload on staff can lead to burnout and low morale. Approaches like Lean, DevOps and Kanban emphasise a focus on managing the flow of work.

Kanban (meaning signboard or billboard in Japanese) is a scheduling system for lean manufacturing and just-in-time manufacturing (JIT). Taiichi Ohno, an industrial engineer at Toyota, developed Kanban to improve manufacturing efficiency. Kanban is one method to achieve JIT. The system takes its name from the cards that track production within a factory. **Lean thinking** has its roots in lean production, which is defined as "an assembly-line methodology developed originally for Toyota and the manufacturing of automobiles. It is also known as the Toyota Production System or just-in-time production. Lean production principles are also referred to as lean management or lean thinking." Lean IT is the application of lean production principles to service providers, specifically to the development and management of IT products and services.

Prioritising work

Effective prioritisation can help to manage the flow of work and make sure queues don't build up. All work needs to be prioritised, including:

- Requests;
- Defects;
- Projects; and
- Improvement opportunities.

Prioritisation techniques include swarming and triage. Low-priority work has to wait until high- and medium-priority work has been completed. Triage can be used to manage workloads such as development backlogs and incident queues. However, it's important to make sure the low-priority work doesn't get overlooked.

Options for service delivery

Some of the options for service delivery include:

- Buy vs build considerations;
- Sourcing options; and
- Service integration and management.

Roles in sourcing

The service provider has the option of engaging a third party for service components or creating the service components themselves. Service components can refer to people, tools, information, or any other resource necessary for service creation, delivery or support.

It's important to differentiate between a partner, supplier and vendor.

- Partner: *"A partner is an organization that provides products and services to consumers and works closely with its consumers to achieve common goals and objectives."*
- Supplier: *"A supplier is an organization that provides products and services to consumers but does not have goals or objectives in common with its consumers."*
- Vendor: *"'Vendor' is a generic term used to describe any organization that sells a product or service to a customer. From the service consumer's perspective, a vendor can either be a partner or a supplier, or it can*

have no direct service relationship with the service consumer. A vendor can also be a partner in some areas and a supplier in others."

Buy vs build considerations

It's rare for a service provider to create products and services using only their own resources. An objective decision must be made about whether to build or buy service components. A clear sourcing strategy will support these decisions. The strategy guides decision-making by collecting data about areas including:

- Current and future sourcing needs;
- Current and future costs of sourcing the components;
- Resource availability;
- Viability of current suppliers and any barriers preventing emerging suppliers; and
- Risks and costs of multi-sourcing.

Once a sourcing strategy is in place, organisations must realise and mitigate potential biases due to previous experience with a product or vendor, pressure from aggressive sales agents, pressure from management to reduce costs, and even 'shiny object' syndrome (the desire to work with something just because it's new).

The table below shows some of the considerations for build or buy decisions.

Table 15: Build or Buy?

Build the service component in-house	Buy the service component
Service component relies heavily on organisation-specific knowledge	Scarce in-house resources
Customer demands personalisation	Creating the component is predictable and repetitive
Service environment is volatile (customer can change provider with little financial impact, change business models, etc.)	Skills/competencies to create, operate and support are highly specialised and need to be developed
Service components are not used across the mass market	Demand for the component is low or subject to variation (holidays, specific events, etc.)
Compliance to standards	Components are highly commoditised

"We can build that; it will only take a few days!".
Brilliant! But what about support, maintenance and future
development? Building things internally may be quicker
and cheaper at first, but as Banksbest found with the
Bizbank system, the full lifecycle of a product or service
must be considered. I've experienced this issue myself
with some plug-ins that we developed. They worked
perfectly, but the small organisation we purchased them
from didn't have the resources to provide us with support
when we needed it.

Requirements for service components should reflect the
needs of all relevant stakeholders and not focus solely on
functionality. Other requirements include the maintainability
of the component, location of the vendor, cultural alignment,
vendor brand image, and others.

One way to prioritise requirements is to use a MOSCOW
analysis:

- **Must have** – mandatory requirement.
- **Should have** – should be included, if possible.
- **Could have** – requirements that could be included as
  long as they don't impact the higher priority ones.
- **Won't** – requirements not included at this time but may
  be added in the future.

Once the requirements are defined, select a vendor if they are being sourced externally. This is normally done using a request for quote (RFQ), request for proposal (RFP) or request for information (RFI):

- RFQ: *"This technique is used when requirements have been defined and prioritized, and the organization needs information on:*
  - *how vendors might meet requirements*
  - *how much it might cost to meet the published requirements."*
- RFP: *"This technique is used when the problem or challenge statement has been clearly articulated, but the exact requirements or specifications of the service components are unclear or likely to change. Vendors need to provide recommendations or potential solutions, articulating benefits and outcomes as well as costs."*
- RFI: *"This technique is used when requirements are unclear or incomplete and external assistance is needed to refine or add requirements. RFIs are often followed by an RFQ or RFP."*

Sourcing options

As part of the sourcing strategy, organisations will have a defined sourcing model. This model describes:

- Conditions where a service provider will source components;
- Roles and responsibilities of the vendor;
- Performance assessment criteria of the vendor;
- Management policies; and

- Financial policies.

Common types of sourcing include insourcing, outsourcing, onshore, nearshore and offshore:

- Insource: *"Where the organization's existing resources are leveraged to create, deliver, and support service components."*
- Outsource: *"Where the organization transfers the responsibility for the delivery of specific outputs, outcomes, functions, or entire products or services to a vendor."*
- Onshore: *"Vendors are in the same country."*
- Nearshore: *"Vendors are located a different country or continent, but there is a minimal difference in time zone."*
- Offshore: *"Vendors are located in a different country or continent, often several time zones away from the organization."*

Service integration and management

As organisations use an increasing number of suppliers, the difficulty of managing and integrating the many suppliers into the value stream can impact the overall value delivery. Service integration and management (SIAM) is an approach where a single entity manages the delivery of all outsourced products and services.

ITIL 4 defines four SIAM models:

- Retained service integration: *"Where the retained organization manages all vendors and coordinates the service integration and management function itself."*
- Single provider: *"Where the vendor provides all services as well as the service integration and management function."*
- Service guardian: *Where a vendor provides the service integration and management function, and one or more delivery functions, in addition to managing other vendors."*
- Service integration as a service: *"Where a vendor provides the service integration and management function and manages all the other suppliers, even though the vendor does not deliver any services to the organization."*

Figure 11[20] demonstrates the four ITIL SIAM models:

---

[20] *ITIL® 4: Create, Deliver and Support,* figure 5.2. Copyright © AXELOS Limited 2020. Used under permission of AXELOS Limited. All rights reserved.

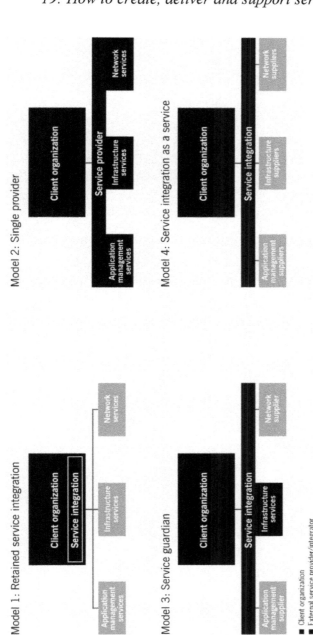

Figure 11: Service integration models

More information about SIAM can be found in *Service Integration and Management (SIAM™) Foundation Body of Knowledge (BoK), Second edition* and *Service Integration and Management (SIAM™) Professional Body of Knowledge (BoK), Second edition:*

- *www.itgovernancepublishing.co.uk/product/service-integration-and-management-siam-foundation-body-of-knowledge-bok-second-edition.*
- *www.itgovernancepublishing.co.uk/product/service-integration-and-management-siam-professional-body-of-knowledge-bok-second-edition.*

More information about SIAM is also available on the Scopism website:

www.scopism.com.

CHAPTER 20: EXAM PREPARATION

Here are the key facts about the ITIL 4 Create, Deliver and Support (CDS) exam:

- The exam is 90 minutes long. Extra time is allowable if English is not your native language and a translated paper isn't available.
- The exam is closed book – it's just you and your knowledge.
- It has 40 multiple choice questions, and you must get 28 correct, or 70% to pass.
- There is no negative marking (so you don't lose a mark if you get a question wrong).
- There are 13 questions at Bloom's Level 2 and 27 at Bloom's Level 3.

Remember, this is a Specialist course, and is part of the Managing Professional stream.

Your training provider for the ITIL 4 Specialist Create, Deliver and Support course will provide you with access to at least one sample exam. When you're ready to attempt the sample paper, try to reproduce, as far as possible, the conditions of the real exam.

Set aside 90 minutes to complete the paper and make sure there are no distractions: don't make a coffee; don't raid the refrigerator; don't check your emails … or Facebook … or Twitter; switch off your phone.

If you don't focus exclusively on the sample exam questions, you will not have a good indication of your possible performance in the live exam. Your sample exam may highlight areas for further study before you take your final exam.

Here are some good practices for taking multiple choice exams:

Manage your time: if you're stuck on a question, mark it and go back to it later. It's easy to spend too long staring at one question, but there may be easier marks to be picked up further on in the paper.

Have a technique: I like to go through an exam and complete all the questions I feel confident about. That allows me to see how many of the more challenging ones I need to get right to have a successful result.

Trust your instinct: one of the most common bits of exam feedback is delegates who wish they had not changed their answer at the last minute. It's fine to check over what you've done but be very wary about making changes in those last few seconds.

Use the process of elimination: each question has four possible answers – if you can discount one or two of them, then you've dramatically increased your odds of picking the right answer.

Don't panic! If your mind goes blank, move on and look at another question – you can do this with online and paper exams. Your subconscious mind will work away even when you're answering a different question.

Read the question carefully: if you're not careful, you will answer the question you **think** you see, not the one that's actually there.

And that's all from me! I hope you've enjoyed the book, and that the extra content I've provided will help you to start using ITIL 4 CDS concepts in your own role. You can find me on LinkedIn and Twitter – I'd love to hear if you've enjoyed the book and how your studies and your ITIL qualification help you in your career.

- *www.linkedin.com/in/claireagutter/*
- *https://twitter.com/ClaireAgutter*

APPENDIX A: BANKSBEST CASE STUDY

Company overview

Banksbest was originally HW Banking. It was founded in 1953 in the UK and has branches in most major UK cities. It focuses mainly on business clients, but it also has a mortgage department that offers residential mortgages to aspiring homeowners and buy-to-let mortgages to landlords.

The Banksbest board of directors initiated a digital transformation programme in 2017. At the same time, a new CEO and a new CIO were recruited. A Chief Digital Officer (CDO) role has also been established. As part of the digital transformation programme, the bank rebranded from HW Banking to Banksbest, which was seen as a more customer-focused brand.

Banksbest has defined these strategic goals:

- To be the tenth largest provider of business banking services in the UK (growing its customer base by approximately 25%).
- To grow its residential mortgage business by 50%.
- To build a reputation as a 'digital first' banking provider.

There is some conflict during board meetings, as the CFO is not fully convinced about the value of the CDO role and the digital transformation programme. She would prefer to focus on cost management.

Bankbest's head office and data centre are in Manchester. The customer service centre is in Reading. There is also an agreement with a business process outsourcing company in

Bulgaria, Employeez on Demand, that provides additional customer service resources during peak times. The customer service centre operates seven days a week, between 8:00 am and 6:00 pm, and support is also available via the bank's website on a 24x7 basis.

Banksbest's 50 branches are open Monday to Saturday, between 9:00 am and 5:00 pm.

Banksbest has a good reputation in a competitive field. However, the rebrand has confused some customers, and the digital transformation programme has not delivered many measurable results yet. Banksbest needs to improve its online services and embed its new brand in order to grow.

Company structure

Banksbest employs 700 staff. 400 of them work in the bank's branches, 100 in the call centre and 200 in the head office and support functions. Additional staff are supplied by Employeez on Demand during peak times.

Banksbest is split into divisions:

- Central Operations – provides support services for all departments. Operations includes HR, Finance, Marketing and IT. The IT department has 50 staff.
- Customer Services – includes the staff who work in and manage the customer service centre, as well as some technical specialists who work on the systems used in the customer service centre.
- Branches – responsible for the branches providing face-to-face banking services. The branches are expensive to maintain but offer an in-person service that some Banksbest customers value.

The digital transformation programme is being run by a digital team that operates outside the existing divisions.

Future plans

To achieve its goals, Banksbest and the digital transformation programme team are working on a number of different initiatives. This includes the flagship 'My Way' project, which will allow business banking customers to access services however suits them best. Commissioned by the CDO and led by a product owner, My Way will allow business banking customers to use a range of devices to manage their accounts and move seamlessly between branch-based and online transactions. The current plans include:

- Testing biometrics, including fingerprint and voice login, to support My Way;
- My Deposit My Way, a service allowing cheques to be paid in using the camera on a mobile phone; and
- Monitoring customer feedback, levels of demand, and which products are most popular.

After three months, the product owner will report back to the CDO. At this point, the project will either be allocated additional funding, will pivot or will be closed down. My Way is being measured on both governance and compliance and customer satisfaction outcomes.

IT services

All of the IT services are run from the head office and the Manchester data centre. Since the digital transformation programme started, more services are Cloud-hosted by external providers. The main IT services are:

Bizbank – the banking system used in the branches and customer service centre. This system contains customer account information and history, including current and savings accounts. Bizbank is hosted in the Manchester data centre, but there are plans to move it to a Cloud hosting service to improve its resilience. Bizbank incidents sometimes take a long time to resolve because the original developers have left, and documentation is poor.

Mortbank – the mortgage system used in branches and the customer service centre. As well as tracking existing mortgages, Mortbank has a credit-checking facility that supports mortgage approvals. Mortbank was developed by MortSys, which provides ongoing support and maintenance. MortSys is a small organisation and doesn't always respond within its agreed target times.

Mibank – an online self-service portal being developed as part of the My Way project. Mibank allows customers to check their accounts, move money between accounts, pay bills and receive cheques. The functionality of Mibank will expand as the My Way project progresses.

Banksec – Banksec is an identity checking utility that is used by Bizbank, Mortbank and Mibank. Banksec uses two-factor authentication, and biometric capabilities are in development.

IT department

The IT department includes 50 staff split into 4 departments, under the CIO:

- Strategic Planning and Business Relationship Management
- Service Management

- Development
- Operations (including Service Desk)

IT has a good reputation generally, but business staff see the IT department as responsible for day-to-day operations and fixing things. The IT department's development role is less well understood. There is also some friction between the digital transformation programme staff and IT staff.

IT service management

Service management does not have a high profile in Banksbest.

The CIO holds a position at board level, and likes to be seen as dynamic and responsive, rather than process driven and bureaucratic. However, some recent service outages have led to a level of interest in service management best practices, as well as assessment of other ways of working including DevOps, Agile and Lean.

There are some culture issues in the IT department, including an 'us and them' attitude that means developers and operations staff don't always work well together.

Sample employee biographies

Lucy Jones	Lucy joined Banksbest as a graduate trainee five years ago. As part of her training, she spent six months in each of the major departments (Central Operations, Branches and Customer Services). During her time in Central Operations, she spent two months in Finance, two months in HR and two months in IT, including working on the service desk.

	After completing her graduate trainee programme, Lucy was offered a job in HR, and worked there for three years. She was then offered a newly created role of Product Owner and is now responsible for the My Way project. Lucy has a good understanding of the Banksbest business units and the IT services that support them.
Doug Range	Doug has worked for Banksbest for 20 years, since it was HW Banking. He started work as counter staff in one of the branches and worked his way up to branch manager. His branch was chosen to be one of the pilot locations for the rollout of Bizbank some years ago, and for two years he acted as a super-user for this system, logging the queries he handled onto the service desk system. He has recently been promoted to a head office role, including training the customer service centre staff.

Doug is working with Lucy on the My Way project, helping to provide customer intelligence, and ensuring the customer service centre staff are kept up to date. |

FURTHER READING

IT Governance Publishing (ITGP) is the world's leading publisher for governance and compliance. Our industry-leading pocket guides, books, training resources and toolkits are written by real-world practitioners and thought leaders. They are used globally by audiences of all levels, from students to C-suite executives.

Our high-quality publications cover all IT governance, risk and compliance frameworks and are available in a range of formats. This ensures our customers can access the information they need in the way they need it.

Our other publications about ITIL include:

- *ITIL® 4 Essentials – Your essential guide for the ITIL 4 Foundation exam and beyond, second edition* by Claire Agutter, *www.itgovernancepublishing.co.uk/product/itil-4-essentials-your-essential-guide-for-the-itil-4-foundation-exam-and-beyond-second-edition*
- *ITIL® 4 Direct, Plan and Improve (DPI) – Your companion to the ITIL 4 Managing Professional and Strategic Leader DPI certification* by Claire Agutter, *www.itgovernancepublishing.co.uk/product/itil-4-direct-plan-and-improve-dpi*
- *ITIL® 4 High-velocity IT (HVIT) – Your companion to the ITIL 4 Managing Professional HVIT certification* by Claire Agutter,

www.itgovernancepublishing.co.uk/product/itil-4-high-velocity-it-hvit

For more information on ITGP and branded publishing services, and to view our full list of publications, visit *www.itgovernancepublishing.co.uk*.

To receive regular updates from ITGP, including information on new publications in your area(s) of interest, sign up for our newsletter at *www.itgovernancepublishing.co.uk/topic/newsletter*.

Branded publishing

Through our branded publishing service, you can customise ITGP publications with your company's branding.

Find out more at

www.itgovernancepublishing.co.uk/topic/branded-publishing-services.

Related services

ITGP is part of GRC International Group, which offers a comprehensive range of complementary products and services to help organisations meet their objectives.

For a full range of resources on ITIL visit *www.itgovernance.co.uk/shop/category/itil*.

Training services

The IT Governance training programme is built on our extensive practical experience designing and implementing management systems based on ISO standards, best practice and regulations.

Our courses help attendees develop practical skills and comply with contractual and regulatory requirements. They also support career development via recognised qualifications.

Learn more about our training courses in ITIL and view the full course catalogue at *www.itgovernance.co.uk/training*.

Professional services and consultancy

We are a leading global consultancy of IT governance, risk management and compliance solutions. We advise businesses around the world on their most critical issues and present cost-saving and risk-reducing solutions based on international best practice and frameworks.

We offer a wide range of delivery methods to suit all budgets, timescales and preferred project approaches.

Find out how our consultancy services can help your organisation at *www.itgovernance.co.uk/consulting*.

Industry news

Want to stay up to date with the latest developments and resources in the IT governance and compliance market? Subscribe to our Weekly Round-up newsletter and we will send you mobile-friendly emails with fresh news and features about your preferred areas of interest, as well as unmissable offers and free resources to help you successfully start your projects. *www.itgovernance.co.uk/weekly-round-up*.